The Educated Student

The Educated Student

Getting the Most Out of Your College Years

Richard Labunski, Ph.D., J.D.

Marley and Beck Press
Versailles

The Educated Student: Getting the Most Out of Your College Years
Copyright © 2003 by Richard Labunski

Publisher's Cataloging-in-Publicatioon
(Provided by Quality Books, Inc.)

Labunski, Richard E.
    The educated student : getting the most out of your college years / Richard Labunski. -- 1st ed.
        p. cm.
    Includes index.
    LCCN 2002103559
    ISBN 0-9677498-8-3

    1. College student orientation.   I. Title.

LB2343.3.L33 2002   378.1'98
                                     QBI02-200322

Quantity discounts are available on bulk purchases of this book. For information, contact the publisher:

Marley and Beck Press
P.O. Box 824
Versailles, KY 40383
www.marleyandbeck.com
info@marleyandbeck.com

First Edition
10 9 8 7 6 5 4 3 2 1

Interior design and composition by Publishing Professionals, New Port Richey, FL.
Cover design by George Foster

Printed and bound in the United States.

For Elisa

Table of Contents

Acknowledgments

Several people were generous with their time and made substantial contributions to the preparation of this book. Mike Farrell, a colleague in the School of Journalism and Telecommunications and a Ph.D. candidate, demonstrated his usual patience and skill as he carefully reviewed the manuscript. His comments and criticisms were very helpful.

Karla Salmon Robinson, Ph.D., a former colleague in the School, made many suggestions that were incorporated into the manuscript. I am grateful for their encouragement and assistance.

Oliver Brooks, a bright and articulate high school senior, also made some very useful comments.

As with all my writing projects, no one worked as hard at helping to improve the manuscript as my wife, Elisa. She assisted at every phase by suggesting the idea for the book, offering comments about chapter topics and content, and in proofreading tirelessly. I dedicate this book to her with my admiration, gratitude, and love.

During my more than 20 years of teaching at universities, I have learned a lot from my students. That experience is reflected in many of these pages. I hope this book will help high school and college students to get as much as they can out of their college years. I know I am still enjoying mine.

Introduction and Author's Note

Going to college is one of the most exciting and interesting things you will ever do. You will probably work hard and face numerous challenges, but if you know how to approach college the right way, you will learn a lot and have fun at the same time.

You and your parents may have sacrificed for years so you can attend a good school. You may have studied extra hours instead of doing things with your friends so you could get better grades. You may have worked at jobs throughout high school and beyond to save money for tuition and expenses. Your parents may have skipped vacations or other pleasures to put money in your college fund.

Your parents want you to enjoy your college years, but they also know that you will likely face a competitive job environment after you graduate and that you must get everything you can from your undergraduate education.

Because college is so important for your career and life, you may have already looked at one of the many college guides that are available. Some include advice on dealing with homesickness, finding the right roommate, and having a good social life.

This book is different. It focuses on the academic side of the college experience. That may not sound as much fun as reading about where to find the best parties, but it is far more important. This book can help you get the most out of your classes and your professors. College involves a variety of social and educational experiences, but what you learn from your courses and how you make that learning last beyond graduation day is what really matters.

Because you have so much at stake, this book may be among the most important you and your parents ever read. If you rely on the information and advice offered here, you will make decisions that could profoundly affect your undergraduate studies and your career.

This book is not about how to get high grades, although much of what is discussed here can improve your grades. Good grades and learning are *not* the same. Just because you get an "A" or a "B" in a course does not mean you are learning what you should. You can earn an "A" in a class and learn very little, while receiving a "C" in a course that inspires you.

A good grade point average will help with getting into graduate or professional schools and may get you an interview with some employers. But if you approach every course with the attitude that you will only do what is required for the exams, you will have missed much of what college has to offer.

Four years or more of undergraduate study sound like a long time, but they go by quickly. You will meet many different people such as teachers, advisers, classmates, roommates, sorority sisters and fraternity brothers, people you work with at a job, and prospective employers at internships. Some of those people may become lifelong friends, while others may be important contacts for your career.

You will be exposed to subjects you didn't know anything about and didn't think you would be interested in, only to find that they are not only engaging and stimulating, but have also helped you choose a career. The reverse may also happen. You may have thought you knew what you wanted to do with your future but after taking courses in the field, you want to do something else.

When you have graduated and are working, you will think about the good times you had as a student. Although you obviously can't know how you will feel about college later on, you can take steps now to make your undergraduate years rewarding.

Who Should Read this Book?

High school juniors and seniors, college students, and parents will benefit the most from this book. High school teachers and guidance counselors, and college professors and administrators, will also find valuable information here.

Success in college involves much more than taking notes in a lecture and memorizing material for exams. If a university education is to have lasting value, you must develop the abilities to think critically, to deal with challenging situations, and to write and speak well. Without those skills, you will find that college was little more than an expensive way to meet interesting people.

How to get good academic advice, choose classes, get the most out of every course, balance your classes with other activities, select a major, take notes, study for exams, write papers, and keep grades in perspective, are among the topics covered here.

Another section of this book explains how to develop the right kind of relationship with your professors. Although you will learn much on your own, professors play an essential role in determining what you get out of your courses and the experience of going to college. Besides teaching course material, professors should help you develop the long-term skills necessary to succeed in a career and have a fulfilling life. But professors can't do that without your active involvement.

Finding the right place to study, extra-curricular activities, and having an impact on your school are also discussed.

The final section considers legal issues. You and your parents should know something about the rights and responsibilities that go with being a student. You may face many situations on and off campus that could lead to serious consequences. Learning about the legal environment in which you study and live could reduce the chances that something will go wrong.

AUTHOR'S NOTE:
MY BACKGROUND

> This book recommends that you approach your college years in a particular way. You need to have confidence in the person who is offering the advice you find here.

I have been a professor for more than 20 years and have taught at the following universities:

- University of California, Santa Barbara (2 years while a graduate student)
- University of Nevada, Reno (1 year)
- Penn State University (2 years)
- University of Washington (11 years)
- University of Kentucky (7 years to date)

At California and Nevada, I was a faculty member in political science departments. I taught a variety of classes including American government, constitutional law, judicial process, American presidency, and mass media and politics.

At Penn State, Washington and Kentucky, I have been on the faculty of communications or journalism schools. Among the courses I have taught are introduction to journalism, broadcast news writing, radio/TV news reporting, mass media law, government and the media, and new media technology. I also have supervised student-produced TV newscasts shown on cable.

I am currently an associate professor in the School of Journalism and Telecommunications at the University of Kentucky.

I have taught more than 6,000 students from first semester freshmen to students in M.A. and Ph.D. programs. My classes have had as many as several hundred students and as few as five.

I have also given academic and career advice to several thousand students over the years. At most of the universities where I have worked, students must see an academic adviser, usually a professor, before they can register for classes for the next semester. I have counseled many students about their career plans and occasionally helped with personal problems.

Not only have I taught university students, I spent some years as one myself and that helps me see things from a student's perspective. I studied journalism and government for three years at American University in Washington, D.C., then later transferred to the University of California, Berkeley, where I completed a B.A. in political science in 1975. At the University of California, Santa Barbara, I finished an M.A. in political science in 1977 and a Ph.D. in political science in 1979. I was also president of the graduate students association at California. I later attended law school and completed a J.D. at Seattle University School of Law in 1994.

A NOTE ABOUT COMPUTERS

Computers are an important part of education today. You should buy a computer to take with you to college or if you commute, to have one at home. You may think that spending $1,000 or more on a computer is a lot, especially when college campuses operate computer labs, but you will be glad you bought one. Considering what you will spend on tuition, books, transportation, and living expenses, the relative cost of a good computer is worth it.

Almost all universities offer good computer facilities on campus. Computer labs are almost always open until late in the evening or even 24 hours a day. They give students the chance to do assignments, send and answer e-mail, and explore Web sites using advanced software and high-speed telephone lines.

Because so much of your interaction with the university will be through computers, you need one for your dorm room or off-campus home. Professors frequently communicate with students individually and as a class through e-mail. They often make assignments that require students to use Internet resources. You will write all your research papers and do other assignments on a computer. Having your own computer will allow you to stay in touch with your professors and work on assignments without having to be in the computer labs.

Part I

1

Advising and Choosing Courses

Summary: This chapter discusses academic advising, requirements for a degree, why you are responsible for your academic program, and how to get into the classes you need.

Why It Matters: Choosing the right courses at the right time is essential if you are to graduate on time and get the most out of college.

The first weeks at college can be overwhelming. You have to find the buildings where your classes will be held and locate professors' offices. If there is a problem with your financial aid or housing situation, you will have to deal with that. Although you probably pre-registered, you may have to drop a course or add another, only to find that the classes you need are filled. While all this is going on you will be meeting people, trying to study, going to parties and athletic events, and perhaps learning to live on your own for the first time.

Despite the distractions, you should remember the reason you are at a university is to learn, and you will do most of that learning in your courses. Every class you take is important.

You may believe that because you have four years ahead of you, you don't have to worry if you take a few classes that don't count toward your major or turn out not to be beneficial. That is not the case. You will be surprised at how few courses you end up taking while an undergraduate, especially in your major. There is little room for error.

It is not always easy to schedule the courses you need. Later in this chapter, you will learn how to increase your chances of getting the right classes. You have to be assertive about this. You may be competing with many other students.

The process of helping you plan your academic program begins even before you are enrolled, at the summer advising conference, and then continues in advising sessions until graduation.

**Getting good academic
advice is essential, and you need
to be actively involved in the process.**

Who Is Responsible for Your Academic Program?

There is a misconception on the part of many students and parents that should be cleared up right away. You and your parents may believe that it is an adviser's responsibility to make sure that you are taking the right classes so you can get into the major you want and graduate on time. It is not. It is *your* responsibility. There are often too many students and too few advisers for them to be able to closely monitor your progress as you go through your program of study.

At my university, two advisers in our college are responsible for more than a thousand students. While professors handle much of the advising of juniors and seniors, many students need to see these advisers throughout their undergraduate years. With 500 students for each adviser, you can imagine how difficult it is for them to keep track of all of the students' progress over a period of several years.

One way advisers try to help students plan their program is to provide information in written form. Such documents are likely to tell you what the requirements are in the college or department, when courses are offered, what electives are offered inside and outside the college, and other important information.

The problem is that some students don't read those documents carefully. If they did, they would be less likely to take courses in the wrong order or misunderstand the college or department requirements. Be sure to keep all the written information you get from advisers. You should also take notes when you meet with an adviser so you will have a record of what was said.

The advising guide given to students and parents attending my university's 2002 summer conference clearly explains that you must play an active role in understanding the requirements and making sure they are being met. Similar information can be found in the university's general bulletin. Although academic advisers are an important part of the system, the statements from the summer guide clearly show that students bear most of the responsibility for planning their studies. This is what it says in part:

Students are responsible for:

a. knowing the requirements of their particular program; selecting courses that meet those requirements in an appropriate time frame; and monitoring their progress toward graduation;

b. consulting with appropriate advisers designated to handle the kind of questions or concerns they have;

c. scheduling and keeping academic advising appointments in a timely manner throughout their academic career, so as to avoid seeking advising only during busy registration periods; and

d. being prepared for advising sessions.

Advisers are responsible for:

a. helping students clarify their options, goals and potential, and understand themselves better;

b. helping students understand the nature and purpose of a college education;

c. providing accurate information about the educational options, requirements, policies and procedures; and

d. helping students plan educational programs and monitor and evaluate their educational progress.

Summer Advising Conference

Most universities schedule one- or two-day advising conferences during the summer before your freshman year. These meetings are mandatory, although students who cannot attend may be able to go to an abbreviated session just before classes start so they can register for their first courses. At the summer conferences you will learn about the university's requirements, and you will sign up for your first classes.

In most universities, you will hear initially from people who talk about issues that affect all students. Then, if you know what your major is likely to be, you will be assigned to groups led by advisers from that college or department. (Universities are usually divided into "colleges." This should not be confused with the word "college" when it describes the whole institution). If you are unsure of your major, you will meet advisers from a central university office who will tell you about the university's general education requirements and about academic programs on campus.

Summer conferences cover a variety of issues such as graduation requirements, registering for classes, living in the dorm, buying meal tickets, financial aid, computer facilities, and health care. You may also have the opportunity to take placement exams that will allow you to skip some classes. Tours of the campus are also provided.

Many parents go to these meetings and that is a good idea. Your parents should be knowledgeable about the university you will be attending. You may need their advice about courses or majors or other issues related to the learning or living environment you will encounter. Although it is great to have the freedom of being in college, you should include your parents in important decisions related to your education.

Advisers who run the summer conferences like parents to be there for another reason. These sessions convey so much information in such a short time that you will likely suffer from information overload. Parents can help take notes and remember important things that were said. Advisers say parents often ask good questions because they may have been to college and remember some of the things they needed to know as they started their undergraduate studies.

Central Advising

During your first year or two at a university, you are likely to get academic advice from advisers who see students from throughout the university. Those advisers work very hard under difficult circumstances. They often have to deal with a huge number of students. They have to know the requirements that all university students must meet in addition to being familiar with what every program on campus expects of its students.

You have to be sure that the information you get from central advising is complete and up to date. Sometimes departments informally modify their requirements without getting the approval of the university and thus the central advisers have no way of knowing that things have changed. You should double-check advice you get about college or major requirements or programs. You can do this by talking to an adviser in the department or a professor.

You also have to watch out for the reverse of this situation. Professors may understand their own department's requirements, but they often know less about the general education requirements. If you have doubts, don't accept a professor's advice about university requirements at face value. Check with an adviser.

**Always double-check
the advice you are getting
about what courses are required.**

You need to take responsibility for your academic program by reading the information given to you at advising conferences, in the bulletin and schedule of classes, and by your adviser. Once you have read that information carefully, you will be in a better position to judge the accuracy of the advice you are getting.

What Classes to Take and When

If you go to a university with two semesters in an academic year, you will probably take around 10 courses per year (five each in fall and spring) or 40 for your entire academic career. If your university is on a quarter system, you will probably take 12 courses per year (four each in fall, winter and spring) or 48 courses before graduating. (This assumes you are attending full-time).

It is not enough to know the requirements. You need to know when certain courses should be taken. Classes may be required for graduation, but they may not be offered every semester. If you wait until the end to take a required class and that course is not being taught then, you will not graduate with your classmates. Instead, you will be back in summer, or more likely, fall, to take that one class. That is why it is so important to plan ahead.

Here is a general description of required classes:

University requirements

About half of the credits you take will be part of the university's curriculum, sometimes called "general education" or "distribution" requirements. Everyone must complete these classes.

Universities offer such courses because they want to expose you to the full range of knowledge. Educators believe that you should know something about the physical and social sciences, develop strong writing and speaking skills and an appreciation for English literature, have some capacity for reading and speaking a foreign language, and acquire some math ability. The United States lags behind many developed nations when it comes to math and science skills, and universities believe all students need exposure to those subjects regardless of your eventual major and career plans.

General education courses also involve studying different cultures. That is why you will probably choose courses on developing or Third World nations, or countries that have a different political and cultural history.

College requirements

As mentioned before, most universities are divided into "colleges," and when you eventually choose a major, you will

usually be part of a college that will have its own requirements. For example, if you are a political science major, you
will be in a college of liberal arts or a college of arts and sciences. If you are majoring in biology, you will be in a college
of physical sciences or some similar name.

Sometimes, colleges add additional classes to the university requirements, while at other times they require classes
on different subjects. For example, the university may require
one year of a foreign language, while the college requires an
additional year. Or the university may require all students to
take statistics, while the college also requires calculus or
trigonometry.

**You have to pay close
attention to college requirements.
Some departments or colleges will
not accept credits for certain courses that
were offered by another part of the university.**

If you were counting on a course for graduation and find
out your last semester that your college won't accept it, you
may not be able to finish on time. To keep this from happen-
ing, you should go through a "senior check" with an adviser
at least one semester before you are planning to graduate to
make sure you have everything you need.

Major requirements

By the end of your sophomore year or beginning of your
junior year, you will start to take classes in a major, although
you may do so earlier. At most universities, that means you
will be in a school or department such as a School of Architecture, or a Department of Physics.

Out of your entire academic career, you may end up taking only about a dozen classes in your major. That means no more than a quarter of your total credits will be in the courses that are likely to be related directly to your career plans.

The reason you take relatively few classes in your major is that most universities want you to have a broad liberal arts education at the undergraduate level. You are not attending a "trade school." You are going to a university to be introduced to a variety of subjects and to develop communication skills. You cannot concentrate only on the subjects that interest you.

You may want to check to see if your department is accredited. That could affect how many and what types of courses you take. If the major is accredited, a national or regional organization has looked at the department's faculty, budget, facilities, and other aspects of the program, and determined that it meets the organization's standards. It is prestigious to be recognized this way, but it also means that the department has to abide by the accreditation requirements. Those rules may limit how many classes you can take in the major, how many internships you can do, and impact other aspects of your academic program.

Getting Admitted to Your Major

Some departments have their own admission requirements. Students don't always know this when starting college. They assume that once they are accepted to the university, they can choose any major on campus.

Departments limit enrollment because they often don't have enough room for everyone who wants to take their classes. You need to know in advance what the admission standards are for your prospective major.

University budgets for professors and classrooms often grow slowly compared with student enrollment. This situation creates problems in those programs that teach skills classes where enrollment has to be limited. In such classes, students are learning practical skills that are usually directly connected to a career such as computer programming or architecture. Such classes have to be small so professors can give students the personal attention they need to acquire such skills.

When deciding which students to admit, some departments look only at the overall grade point average and how the student did in pre-major courses. Such courses, of which there will probably be two or three, are required of all students before they are accepted to the department. This may be a bit confusing. The department offers the pre-major courses, but just because you complete them does not mean you are admitted to the major. You still have to be accepted into what is usually called "upper division."

In some departments, once you have attained a decent GPA in your overall courses, (usually in the 2.6-3.2 range, B-minus to B-plus), and have taken the pre-major courses and received passing grades, you are admitted to the program.

But other departments are competitive and have much stricter entrance requirements. Some look closely at not only your overall GPA, but carefully scrutinize your grades in the department's pre-major courses. In close cases, if you did well overall but received mediocre grades in the pre-major classes, you may not be accepted.

Think about what this means. You may have decided years ago to pursue a certain career, and you get into a good university. But because you did not receive high enough grades in a few pre-major classes, you can't get into that department. You will then have to major in something else or transfer to another university.

Some departments give you an examination that will be considered along with grades when they make admissions decisions. If you don't do well on the exam, you won't get into the program.

Some majors require you to submit an essay explaining how the major fits with your career goals. If, for example, you are interested in a career that has little to do with what the department offers, you will not be accepted. In borderline cases, how well your essay is written may be as important as what you say about your career plans. Depending on the number of applicants, admissions committees sometimes interview students to see who is worthy of a coveted spot in the program.

This can create havoc with your undergraduate career. Let's say that the minimum GPA for acceptance to a competitive major is 3.3 (a B-plus). You have a 3.1 GPA and meet all other eligibility requirements. To try to get into the department, you keep taking classes to boost the GPA but soon realize that when you already have a lot of credits, each class has little impact on the overall GPA.

Then, the worst happens. Departments with admission requirements usually have not only a GPA requirement, but have also established a maximum number of credits with which you can apply. While you have been struggling to raise your GPA to 3.3, you have also passed the maximum credit limit and can no longer apply for admission to the program. That means you may be in your senior year and need only a few credits to graduate, but you don't have a major. By the time you find a major and complete that department's requirements, you will have been in college at least two or three semesters longer than you expected. And you will be majoring in a subject that may not be what you wanted.

This process does allow for some flexibility. Every department has an appeals procedure where a committee (usually

---

**It is very important that you know
the admission requirements for your major.**

composed of professors) can consider unusual circumstances. But sometimes, no matter how deserving the student, there is no room.

I served as the chair of the undergraduate admissions committee in the School of Communications at the University of Washington for a number of years. Because of inadequate facilities and not enough professors, we had to limit to 20 the number of students who could be admitted to some of our programs. In the advertising sequence, for example, as many as 60 students would apply every term for 20 openings.

We looked at their grades, test scores, letters of recommendations from professors and others, and essays the students wrote about how the program would fit with their career plans. Then we would choose the students who would be admitted. Many more were qualified than just those 20 and we would have welcomed them if we had room, but we had to make difficult decisions.

Find out what the admission requirements are for the major you are interested in. If enrollment is limited, do everything you can to prepare for admission to the program. If you are unsure how the rules work, talk to an adviser or a professor.

Major Electives

Some students are confused about "electives." While you will have some discretion over the selection of courses, you may not be able to choose whatever course you want. Many departments require their students to take certain electives that relate to the major even when they are offered by other programs. You may end up picking classes from a small list. It can sometimes be difficult to schedule those classes because they may be offered at the same time especially if they are in different departments. By planning ahead, you are more likely to get into the elective classes that you want.

Taking Any Course

After you have completed all requirements, you will be able to take a few classes from anywhere in the university. But even here it pays to plan ahead.

Say, for example, that you majored in computer science and expect to spend your career at hi-tech firms. You may have waited until all the requirements are out of the way to take a class on Shakespeare or creative writing or art because you have long been interested in those subjects. Or you want to take a class on Mozart so you can better understand and appreciate his music. These can be described as "life-enriching" classes.

You may find that the English majors get priority registration in the Shakespeare class and the music students in the Mozart class, and you cannot get in. Or, you may find that even if there is room, the professor will not allow non-majors to take the course.

Even in your senior year when you have enough credits to be able to register early compared to students not as far along, you may find that many classes are closed to non-majors. Since departments sometimes turn away their own students because there is not enough room, you can't get in at all.

If there is a class you really want, plan ahead. Contact the professor well in advance of the start of the semester to see what he or she requires for admission to the class. There may be prerequisites that you have to take, or you may be put on a waiting list with priority given to the department's majors. The most popular classes may be hard to get into, and you will have to be assertive.

The Challenge Facing Transfer Students

Transfer students often have a difficult time getting into classes and meeting the requirements for graduation in a timely manner. They often get off to a rough start because by the time they are admitted and are notified of which courses they can transfer, priority registration is over. They then have a hard time getting into the classes they need at the new university.

Some of the classes taken at another college may not transfer. Sometimes students have to show a syllabus from a course at their previous university before the advising office will accept that class.

Students who expect to transfer should always save the syllabi from their courses.

Often transfer students need more than four years to graduate because by the time they get to the new university, they only have a few semesters left in the four years, but they cannot get all the required classes scheduled during those final semesters or quarters. If you transfer or change majors, you will likely be an undergraduate for more than four years.

What You Should Do

Now that you have read about some of the problems you may face when it comes to getting into courses and completing requirements (there will be more about these issues later), you should know what to do.

Some things are easy to accomplish, while others are more difficult. They all have something in common: You should learn about the requirements you will have to satisfy soon after you arrive on campus. You must take the initiative. It is not only good practice for when you compete in a career environment, it will also increase the likelihood that you will get into the courses you need to graduate on time.

Here are a few things to do right away:

- **Save your advising conference packet.** It will contain important information about resources on campus and will include names and phone numbers of people who can help you.
- **Get an undergraduate bulletin for the university.** Check the campus bookstore or registrar's office for the bulletin and carefully read through the section that explains the requirements. Much of the same information is also printed each term in the schedule of classes and may be more up to date than the bulletin.
- **Obtain a campus phone book.** It will be a good way of getting in touch with advisers and professors. Phone books are usually updated each year.
- **Apply for an e-mail account and Internet access.** You will be communicating with faculty, staff and fellow students by e-mail right away and will soon use the Internet for research papers and other assignments.
- **Learn to use the search engine in the university's Web site.** You will find the e-mail addresses and phone numbers of every faculty and staff member at the university. You will often be able to locate the e-mail addresses and phone numbers of other students through the Web site.
- **Find and learn to use the library's Web pages.** You may be amazed at how much information is available online through the library's site. Often, you will have access to a wide range of databases that the university buys for faculty and students.
- **Go to whatever advising sessions are offered.** No matter what time of day they are scheduled, you should attend and take notes. Write down the names of the people presenting the information. Keep those notes in a file. Don't hesitate to ask questions if you don't understand something. Many requirements (university, college and major requirements) are complicated. You will not be the first student to be confused about what science class satisfies the lab requirement or which Spanish class you

need to take if you had three years of Spanish in high school.

- **Go see an adviser.** You need to always be sure that the advice you are getting is accurate and up to date. Advisers at the campus-wide level know the general education requirements well, but they may know less about college and major requirements.

If You Know Your Major

If you are a freshman or sophomore and are thinking about a particular major, you should go to the department and talk with a professor or adviser there about the requirements for getting into the major and what the program is like.

It may not be easy, however, to get that advice. You may not know any of the professors in the department because you haven't taken courses in that major yet, so be persistent. The advisers may be busy with their own students, and they may not want to make time available and will want to send you back to central advising.

Or it is possible there won't be advisers at all. Professors often have to do their own advising, so you will need to see a professor who may already have many advisees in the department.

Learning early on about programs in which you may want to major is important. If you want to graduate in four years, you may need to take the two or three pre-major courses while you are still a freshman and sophomore. Pre-major courses must be taken before you can be admitted to the major. As mentioned before, for departments with separate admissions requirements, grades from these courses will be an important part of the decision whether to admit you.

If you wait until the end of your sophomore year to start the pre-major courses, it will be hard to squeeze all the requirements into the remaining semesters. Some classes will not be offered every term. Some will be filled. Some will be offered at a time that conflicts with another class you have to take. The earlier you choose a major and start taking the pre-major courses, the more likely you will graduate on time.

Don't take all general education requirements in your first two years. Take some classes that relate to your major as well.

You have to decide how many of the university requirements you should take in your first year or so. You could spend much of your first two or three semesters completing general education requirements. You are going to have to take those classes anyway. But it is better to mix those classes with ones that will count toward your major and that may be more interesting to you. If you spend your first few semesters taking nothing but university requirements, those first years won't be as enjoyable as if you had taken a variety of classes.

If You Don't Know Your Major

If you don't know what your major is likely to be, you may not have much choice but to take all general education classes your first two years. You should complete the university requirements as you think about your career plans and what major may interest you.

During your freshman year, talk to a professor in a department where you may want to major. Be persistent no matter how busy professors are. Go to the professor's office hours or make an appointment by e-mail or phone.

As a student, you should be polite but assertive, and don't get discouraged if it takes a little time to arrange a meeting with a professor or the professor doesn't seem to have a lot of time to spend with you. Once you have a meeting scheduled, it may help you to write down some questions to ask before-hand and then take notes during your meeting.

Visiting a class

You should visit one or more classes to help you make a decision. Look at the schedule of classes to see what is offered that semester. Then e-mail or call the professor to say you would like to sit at the back of the classroom and listen to the lecture. Unless there is no space in the room, almost every professor will allow you to attend and will likely talk to you for a few minutes after class.

During that talk, see if the professor will describe the courses in the department and what kinds of jobs students pursue in that major. Or, ask if there is someone in the de-partment you could talk to about those matters.

If you enjoyed the class and thought the professor was in-teresting, that is great. But if you didn't find either the course material or the professor especially engaging, you should visit another class with a different professor. You should not make a decision as important as what your major will be based on one class visit and one professor.

You must take the initiative in gathering information about possible majors.

Go to advising sessions; read about the requirements for the university and departments; seek out a professor or adviser within a department; and do this in your first year even while you are still working on the general education requirements.

Being Assertive

An experienced adviser recently said that in the last few years, she had seen a decline in student "coping" skills. Students often don't persevere, don't follow-up, and get discouraged too easily. In short, they are not assertive enough when it comes to getting into the classes they want to take.

For example, if a student tries to register for a course through the university's computer system and finds that the class is full, most students will accept that as a final answer and not follow up. If that student e-mails the professor, or even better goes to see the professor in person and asks for an override into the class, many times the professor will make room for that student. Or, at a minimum, the professor may put the student on a waiting list so that if other students who previously registered don't take the class, he or she can be added.

This obviously doesn't always work. For example, some classes require the use of computer labs, so there can only be as many students as there are computers. Someone would have to drop the class for you to get in.

In other situations, you may not have completed the prerequisites for the course that either the university, college, department, or the professor requires, and therefore cannot take the course until you have finished those classes.

If you are eligible to take the class but are having a hard time getting in, check again with the computer system to see if space has become available.

Remember, you are responsible for your academic program. Advisers and professors will help you. But you must make sure you are taking the right courses at the right time to make progress toward your degree. Plan ahead by learning the requirements for the university, college and department. Whenever you get advice about something important, you should probably double-check to make sure it is accurate. If you aren't sure what major is right for you, talk to professors in a department where you think you may want to be. It is such an important decision that it is worth the time to check things out in advance.

2

Getting the Most Out of Every Class

Summary: This chapter discusses how to get the most out of each class even if there are many students and the course is not in your major.

Why It Matters: Not every professor or class will change your career or life, but you should have certain goals in mind for every class you take.

If your university experience is to be as meaningful as possible, you have to get something out of all your courses, even the ones that are outside your major. This chapter focuses on how to approach each class in a way that will benefit you long after graduation.

Before discussing this subject, it is important to talk about a problem that happens to a surprising number of freshmen and sophomores. Instead of taking full advantage of being at a university from the moment they arrive on campus, they waste their first year or two.

> **If you goof off your first few semesters,**
> **it can hurt the rest of your college years**
> **and damage your career prospects.**

Some students can't handle the responsibility and freedom that go with being in college. They go to too many parties, stay up too late, sleep late the next morning, miss class, don't study very much, and generally see the first few semesters as a chance to have fun. Instead of being excited and serious about school right away, they over-indulge in activities that may be enjoyable but have little to do with the reason they are at a university.

Your GPA may never recover from the low grades you receive your first two years. Here are some of the consequences you may face:

- You may not be admitted to the major you want.
- You may not be eligible for scholarships in your junior and senior years because many of them are based all or mostly on GPA.
- You may not get into a graduate or professional school.
- You may not get an interview with an employer who screens applicants by GPA.
- As you earn more credits, each grade impacts less on your average. So even if you get more serious about school after the first few semesters, your GPA may not go up much.

Some students have a tough time the first few semesters for legitimate reasons. It can be difficult to make the adjustment from high school to college. You may be taking hard classes. You may miss your friends and have trouble meeting new people. You may not like your living arrangement.

But that is not what I am talking about. I am referring to students who do not study, who miss class frequently, and who get grades that are much lower than they are capable of because they are not serious about school. Students in that situation often drop classes they are in danger of failing and that almost certainly means they will not graduate in four years.

You need to find the right balance between social activities and your schoolwork. You can enjoy all the great things about being in college and still be committed to succeeding academically. Information here and in the chapters ahead will help you find that balance.

Parents also need to know what you are doing when you are away at college. They obviously should not be calling every night to make sure you are in the dorm room studying. Part of the maturing process in college comes from being able to make decisions about how to spend your time. But if parents see you are getting unusually low grades, they need to talk to you about it. They should not wait until two or three semesters have passed.

What Every Course Should Offer

There is an almost endless variety of courses offered on a college campus. Some classes will be extremely important to your major and directly related to your career plans. You will probably spend extra time on those classes.

Ideally, every class will help you do the following:

- Learn the substantive material in the class.
- Improve your analytical skills, and depending on the course, your writing ability.
- Enhance your knowledge in a way that will stay with you for years.
- Satisfy a university, college, major or pre-major requirement (unless it is one of the times when you can take any class you want).

- Learn more about whether you are in or will be pursuing the major that is right for you.
- Gain something from the professor's personal experience in the field.
- Increase or maintain your enthusiasm for learning.

In the classes that you are excited about or that seem directly related to your major and career, you will be able to more easily succeed at these goals compared with courses you don't consider to be very important. But you should approach every class with the attitude that you want something out of that course that will last well beyond the time you leave college.

It may seem odd at first to discuss how to get the most out of each class before we have talked about how to choose a major, but you will be taking classes beginning your first semester on campus, sometimes well before you decide on a major. You should be thinking about a major beginning in your freshman year because to stay on schedule, you may need to take pre-major courses early on. But don't think that you have to choose a major right away. You usually have until the end of the sophomore year before you must formally declare one.

Importance of the Syllabus

Professors are sometimes amazed at how many students don't read the syllabus carefully. You must read every word of it as soon as the class starts. It will provide essential information about the course that may not be provided anywhere else.

> **Read the syllabus carefully. It is like a "contract" between you and the professor.**

A good syllabus will outline the subjects that will be covered during the semester, what exams and papers will be required and when they are due, and how much each assignment will count toward the final grade. They may also include information on how many classes you can miss before there is a grade reduction, or worse, the assigning of a failing grade. Unless you are notified otherwise, you should assume that the syllabus is an authoritative statement of your obligations in the class.

The syllabus will also include the professor's office hours. These are the hours—usually four to eight per week—where professors are supposed to be in their offices and available to students.

Students who don't read the syllabus and abide by the rules it lays out sometimes face serious problems. I was told recently of a student in our department who had an "A" based on the exams and papers in a class, but who exceeded the number of absences allowed as outlined in the syllabus. That student received a failing grade for the course and wasn't able to graduate that semester.

Although a professor will provide an outline for the class in the syllabus and will usually include information about reading assignments and the dates of exams and deadlines for research papers, things change during the semester. If you have missed a class, you should ask a classmate or the teacher if there were important announcements. If there is a class Web site, they may be posted there. Don't assume that once the professor hands out the syllabus at the beginning of the semester, everything will stay the same.

If the syllabus is not clear or if there is information left out that you think is important, ask the professor to clarify. A good syllabus will cover all of the major issues and because it is in writing, you should not be confused about what is expected.

Importance of Attendance

To get the most out of every course, you should attend every class session. You may get sick or have a family or personal crisis during the semester, but unless there is a legitimate reason, you should always go to class. Here are some of the advantages of attending every class period:

- Much of the course material is covered in class and can't be found in the book.
- The lectures and discussion in class can clarify the book. Sometimes the information in the book is confusing, out of date, or simply wrong.
- Due dates for assignments are all subject to change. The only way to be sure you have the latest information is to attend class and be on time.
- You and your classmates may get a chance to talk about the issues in the course during the class period. That will help you learn the material.
- Regular attendance is an important part of developing a good relationship with your professors.

If the class is large, it may be impossible for the professor to take attendance. So if you don't go to class regularly, no one is likely to know. You may be especially tempted to skip class if it is not required and is on a subject you don't care much about. Don't do it. You'll learn a lot more from being in the class than from reading someone else's notes later.

General Education Classes

As mentioned earlier, about half of the classes you take will be required by the university. The university wants you to be exposed to a broad range of subjects. That is why you will likely take courses in the hard sciences such as biology and chemistry, social sciences such as sociology or political science, humanities classes such as English and history, a foreign language and math.

The challenge of large classes

If you are attending a medium-sized or large university, you may find that some of the general education classes enroll hundreds of students. Some may even have more than a thousand. In such large classes, the professor will be a distant figure on a stage in a huge auditorium, and you will deal almost exclusively with a graduate teaching assistant who will be in charge of your section. (Large lecture classes are divided into groups or sections, each led by a teaching assistant who is usually a graduate student).

Universities want to squeeze as many students into those classes as they can for several reasons. First, it saves money. It costs much less for one professor to teach six hundred students than it does for six professors to teach one hundred students each. And second, because many of those courses are introductions to the subject, universities believe that a good textbook and a professor who is an interesting lecturer are enough to expose you to the material.

Many universities try very hard to make these classes more enjoyable by assigning excellent lecturers as the instructors, by using additional resources such as Web sites and advanced visual aids, and by giving students time to meet in small sections. Don't be discouraged by having to take a freshman or sophomore class with a lot of students. By the time you are a junior, almost all your classes will be smaller.

Even with a large class, you can adopt several strategies to make sure you get the most out of it. In the pages that follow, you will read a discussion of how to make every class meaningful.

The learning environment
in large classes

It takes a dedicated professor to excite hundreds of students in an auditorium day after day. Amazingly, many are able to do that. But it is hardly the ideal environment in which to teach or learn.

Due to the distance between the professor and students in a large classroom or auditorium, it may be difficult to see or hear what is going on. Relatively few students will get the chance to make comments or ask questions during the lecture period. You may feel that you barely know the professor even after an entire semester.

Students don't always recognize the limitations of such an environment and get discouraged. If the professor is not captivating, some students may be less interested in the class, may pay less attention to the lectures, and may attend class less frequently.

What you should understand is that a professor can be less than dynamic and still provide important information that can have lasting impact on your life. Although it may be more enjoyable to listen to the lectures of an animated professor who tells great stories, that does not mean someone who is soft-spoken is not a good teacher.

The contrary may also be true. A professor can be charismatic and funny but provide little substantive information. The class may be entertaining, but except for the professor's amusing anecdotes, you may not remember anything from the course after the final exam.

You should not judge professors and determine how much commitment you make to a class based on how amusing they are. You should go to class every day no matter what time it is offered and listen to the professor carefully as you take notes.

Discussion groups in large classes

If you are in a large freshman or sophomore class, you may attend not only lectures with the professor, but also a section of 20–50 students with a graduate teaching assistant (or TA).

Always go to discussion groups. They are an important part of the learning process.

The TA will answer questions and clarify material from the lectures. If you are in a class with 500 students, there is almost no time in the lectures for questions or comments from the students. But the smaller section will give you the opportunity to discuss the issues in the course with your classmates. Being able to articulate the concepts that you are learning in the class, to question conventional ways of dealing with the subject, or make other comments, are an important part of learning.

Many discussion groups meet on a Friday and sometimes early in the morning. Even if you don't like having Friday classes, go to the discussion groups. Besides helping you understand the material in the class, you may hear from interesting guest speakers who are invited to the discussion sections. You will also have the chance to interact with the teaching assistant who may be an experienced teacher and knowledgeable about the field.

Keep up with the reading

You may decide after a while that you can get by with doing only some of the reading and still do well on the exams. That is not the right way to approach your classes.

When you are just starting college, you may have no idea what subjects will be important to you later either in enriching your life or helping with your career. Read everything that is assigned, and do not leave the reading for the final days before an exam. It is unlikely you will remember much of the material if you have left too many reading assignments to the last minute. More will be said about this in the chapter on preparing for exams.

While taking the class, read at least one thing that is not required

Because of the development of the Internet, this is easy to do. If you are taking a biology class and are studying genes, go to the Internet and look for information about the subject that may be more up to date and, perhaps, more interesting than some of the information in the textbook. This doesn't require a trip to the library. It can be done with your computer.

The reason this is important is you need to make the material in the textbook and the lectures relevant to your life in some way. If not, you may consider the reading to be nothing more than something to study for the exam. By searching Internet resources with the key words you have learned in the class, you may come across scientific knowledge that you find interesting and important. As you learn more about the subject, you will become more sophisticated in searching for material on the Internet.

Try to meet the professor no matter how many students there are

Professors who teach large classes may not appreciate this suggestion. They may believe there are too many students for the professors to meet with them individually.

Let's say the class has 300 students. If each student met with the professor for 15 minutes once during the semester, it would take 4,500 minutes, or 75 hours to see every student in the class. In a 15-week semester, that would mean a professor would have to meet with the students from the one class for five hours a week, every week, to see every student.

Professors often teach three or four classes a semester, and they have a lot of other demands on their time. But very few students from the large lecture classes ever go to a professor's office, so nowhere near 300 students from that class will be competing for the professor's time.

After the first 3–4 weeks of class, e-mail the professor to say you want to come by during office hours to introduce yourself. If you can't come during the professor's office hours, you need to suggest other times, but some professors will not make appointments with students except during those designated hours.

If you make an appointment with the professor during office hours, the professor will likely be there and you may be able to jump ahead of other students who didn't have an appointment.

Find something appropriate from the class to talk to the professor about. Perhaps it is an article you read that you found interesting, or a comment the professor made in class, or the professor's research that you want to ask about. Or, tell the professor that you checked the Internet for current information on a topic the professor discussed and see if the professor is interested in what you found.

Make a point of meeting most of your professors. This may not be easy to do because professors are not always available. They travel out of town, attend a lot of meetings on campus, may have too many students, or they will want you to see the teaching assistant instead unless it is a matter of some urgency.

Why should you make this effort? The reason is that you never know when establishing even a limited relationship with a professor will be beneficial to you. Professors are almost always impressed by students who care enough about the class to make the effort to see them. They are often able to help students in a lot of different ways.

You may be a little intimidated about going to see your professor. Don't assume that the professor's demeanor in the lecture hall will be the same in the office. Because they have so much material to cover, or because of the impersonal environment in which the lectures take place, professors may seem gruff or unfriendly. But they are not likely to be that way in a one-on-one conversation in their office. Students are often surprised to find out how interesting and friendly their professors are as people, something they would never know from the lectures. You'll read more about how to interact with professors later.

Courses That Are Important for Your Career

Although I have encouraged you to get the most out of each of your classes by attending lectures and discussion groups regularly, reading something that updates or makes the course material more relevant, and by meeting the professor, some classes will obviously be more important to you than others.

The pre-major courses or classes in your major are likely to be the most meaningful ones you take in college. You should devote a substantial amount of time to them. You will likely take no more than about a dozen classes in your major. If your major involves courses where you learn practical skills, you may take only a few such classes, and thus each one is extremely important.

Try not to have an especially heavy course load during the semesters you are taking most of the classes in your major. Also, if possible, cut back on the number of hours you work even if that means borrowing money from your parents. Explain to them that these two or three semesters will be among the most important months of your life. How successful you are in your career may depend on how much you learn in those classes.

Making the value of any course last beyond the end of the semester is important for all your classes, but it is especially important for those in your major. This requires a two-pronged approach. While you focus on the material that you need to know for the exams, you also need to think about what you should learn for life after college.

This is difficult to illustrate in the abstract, but think about it this way: Ask yourself, what will likely be on the exams that I need to learn now? And, what can I concentrate on while taking this class that will be important to know for my career?

Approaching classes this way is difficult to do and the professor needs to help you learn for both the short and long term. Sometimes this means you should focus on different subjects within the course, while at other times it means looking at the same subject in different ways. Whatever effort you make to accomplish this will be worth it. After all, this is the primary reason you are in college. You need to stretch your mind so that you can cope with a variety of challenges after you graduate. You also need to learn the substantive material in a way that will stay with you. Your life, and perhaps your career, will benefit greatly from this approach.

Don't make a change based on one course

When you start taking courses that are related to a major you are interested in, you may be tempted to put too much emphasis on a single course, especially if it is the introductory class. If, for example, the first class does not go well, you may think that you have chosen the wrong major and career and that you should do something else. But don't make such an important decision hastily.

Changing majors or rethinking which one you want is too important a decision to be based on one professor or one course. There are always going to be courses and teachers you like a lot, and others you don't. Only if you come to the conclusion that the subject itself is not what you expected, or does not interest you, and you have decided that after taking several courses, should you consider changing your plans for a major.

Learning from the
teacher's personal experience

Depending on the size of the class and the personality of the professor, you can also learn a lot in each course based on the professor's experience in the field. Some professors talk about their research or professional experience in front of the entire class, while others only discuss those subjects individually with a student in the office.

When a professor has professional experience, you will learn things you would not normally get out of the textbook or a formal lecture. When an economics professor talks about working for a think tank and what it was like to advance new economic theories, you may learn about how academic research affects the decisions government makes. When an architecture professor has helped plan an innovative building, he or she can talk about how that project may affect the way such buildings are designed in the future.

Some professors, of course, spend too much time on personal anecdotes that aren't very interesting and don't add much to the class. But when a professor "digresses" this way from the lecture, pay close attention. One of the great things about college is that you get to listen to people who have done interesting things. Your professors are among the best sources of this type of information.

The professor's background or interests may also steer you on a career path you didn't know existed or hadn't thought much about. A single lecture or visit with a professor in the office could have a profound effect on your plans.

Your interest in learning

If you and the professor can make the material relevant in some way to your life and career aspirations, you will have increased your interest and enthusiasm for learning. Each new course should be seen as an adventure. You should never begin a class with the attitude that the material will be boring or irrelevant, or plan to do the minimum that is required to pass the exams.

Make every class an adventure.

You should approach every class with an open mind. Make a commitment to devote the time to the class to make it meaningful and interesting and important. Even if the textbook is not especially exciting, or the professor is not the most dynamic lecturer, find something in the course that you can take with you.

The Cost of Each Class

Besides learning the material, developing new skills, and being inspired by your professors, there is another reason to get the most out of every class. You and your family are likely making a substantial financial commitment to send you to college.

Going to college can be expensive, even if you are attending a public university and paying in-state tuition. When you consider the total cost (tuition, books, living expenses, entertainment, transportation, etc.), each class could be as much as a thousand dollars or more at a public university, or three or four times that amount at a private university.

The cost of each class isn't, of course, the main reason that you need to choose them carefully and make the most of every one. You should take classes on exciting subjects, and with stimulating professors who help prepare you for a career or enrich your life in some way, or both, and increase your enthusiasm for learning.

This chapter should have convinced you that it is important to be serious about school from the moment you arrive on campus, to read the syllabus carefully, to attend class regularly, to explore materials beyond those required for the exams, and to get to know your professors. Make a commitment, especially in the courses related to your career, to get everything you can from your classes.

3

Balancing Classes with Other Activities

Summary: This chapter discusses your course load and how to balance your schoolwork with a job and other activities.

Why It Matters: These decisions will affect not only what you get out of each course and when you will graduate, but may also have an impact on your career.

You may feel pressure from your parents to finish college in four years. Sometimes parents believe so strongly that you should complete your degree within that time that they threaten to cut you off financially if you fall behind. In such a situation, they may no longer pay for your tuition or living expenses. That is a scary prospect for many students who depend on parents to pay tuition bills or to help with books, rent, food, and other expenses.

Universities also want undergraduates to finish in four years. The curriculum and advising systems are set up so a student who plans ahead and takes the right courses at the right time will be able to graduate in eight semesters. College administrators pressure advisers and professors to get students through at an appropriate pace so there is room for the next group of students entering the university.

On the other hand, many universities offer programs that require longer than four years to complete. Some require you to take time off to work in the field. If you study abroad for six or 12 months, you may not be able to graduate in four years. If you do an out-of-town internship, that may delay your graduation because you were unable to take a full course load. If you double-major, that may require an extra semester. By taking some time to consider your options in this area, you will have more control over your schedule and won't be surprised later on.

For those graduating in four years, the following schedule is typical of many universities:

Semesters
- Academic year is fall and spring semesters (approximately 15 weeks each)
- About 120 credits needed to graduate
- Average of 15 credits per semester for eight semesters
- Average of 30 credits per academic year
- If each class is worth three credits, students take five classes each semester

Quarters
- Academic year is fall, winter and spring quarters (approximately 10 weeks each)
- About 180 credits needed to graduate

- Average of 15 credits per quarter for 12 quarters
- Average of 45 credits per academic year
- Most classes will be 4-5 credits; students take four or five classes per quarter

This assumes that you don't take any classes in the summer. If you study during each of the summers beginning with the one following your freshman year, you may be able to graduate one semester early. Sometimes colleges offer relatively few classes in the summer, thus it may be hard to find the ones that you need.

Deciding how many classes to take each semester is not easy, and each student's situation will be different. But there are some things to think about as you plan your course schedule. This is an extremely important decision because it can have an impact not only on your college years, but also on your career.

Working While in College

A substantial number of students have part-time jobs while going to school. I have known many students who worked 15, 20 or 30 hours a week while taking a full-time course load. Some even worked 40 hours a week while struggling to go to college.

Working more than 15 hours a week with a full course load can negatively affect what you get out of college.

If you have to work more than 15 hours a week, you should consider taking fewer courses each semester. That, of course, may mean that you will need longer than four years to graduate. The other option is to maintain a full course load but borrow money so you don't have to work so many hours during the semester.

Balancing class, studying, and your job

If you take a normal course load of five classes, you will most likely be in a classroom about 15 hours a week. But courses are not offered evenly over the five days. Many classes meet Monday and Wednesday, or Tuesday and Thursday. Some classes are offered on Monday, Wednesday and Friday, but many professors don't like to teach on Friday. Therefore, often those 15 hours are spread over just four days.

Assuming that your classes are mostly Monday through Thursday, and you are taking a full load, you will likely be in a classroom about four hours per day.

Many professors expect that for *every hour* of class time, you will do *two hours* of homework. Thus, if you spend 15 hours a week in classes, you will have an additional 30 hours a week of studying. That adds up to 45 hours a week of commitment to school.

Then you have to add the hours from a part-time job. If you work 20 hours a week, you may be at your job during the following time periods:

- 4 hours every weekday (Monday to Friday) or
- 8 hours on Saturday and 8 hours on Sunday, plus 4 hours during the week

If you work more than 20 hours a week, there is even less free time. Here is what this situation looks like for a full-time student with a 20-hour-per-week job:

- Class: 15 hours per week
- Homework: 30 hours per week
- Work: 20 hours per week

This adds up to 65 hours a week or an average of more than *nine hours* a day.

If you are spending more than nine hours in class, studying, and at a part-time job every day, there will be less time to pursue other important and worthwhile activities. You may not be able to work at the campus newspaper or radio station, join a club or organization, get involved in student government, develop hobbies that enrich your life or help your career, or participate in dozens of other activities that make college a fulfilling experience, all because you don't have enough time.

When you are working a lot of hours, you also have less time to make new friends, date, go to parties, or do other social activities that are an important part of the maturing process and which can make college more enjoyable.

Less time for each class

This may be obvious, but it is worth stating clearly: If you are taking a heavy course load and working at a job, you will have less time to devote to each class. For the most part, the more time you spend on a class going to lectures, doing all the reading, checking the Internet for updated and relevant information, perhaps even looking at additional readings that are recommended but not required, the more meaningful the class will be.

**The old maxim is true:
The more time you spend on a
class, the more you will get out of it.**

Even if you were taking a lighter course load and not working, you would not likely devote the same amount of time to each class. Some professors assign more reading, or the reading is more difficult and thus must be done more slowly. Or the teacher requires research papers that take a lot of time to write.

It is, however, a different situation when you *want* to spend more time on a class that interests you or is especially important for your career, and you cannot devote that extra time because you are too busy with your other classes and your job.

There are obviously some part-time jobs where you have the opportunity to study while you are working. But there are not very many like that, and they have a tendency to not pay as well as those that require more active involvement.

Working Fewer Hours While in School

When students work 20 or 25 hours a week, or more, it may seem like their primary activity is their job and going to college is secondary. They only have time to go to class before running off to their jobs. They then study late at night after work when they are tired. Their weekends are taken up with a 10-hour shift waiting tables in a restaurant or bar.

I have known students who had part-time jobs they despised and which some found demeaning. But they had to put up with them because they desperately needed the money.

A "student loan" from your parents

If your parents can afford it, they should provide a "student loan" to you with generous terms so you don't have to work so many hours during the one time in your life when you will be an undergraduate.

It is not hard to see that a small loan from parents (or grandparents or someone else in the family) will save a lot of hours at work.

Here is an example that shows this:

- You earn $6.50 an hour at your part-time job while a student

- You have to work more than 150 hours *before* taxes to make $1,000.
- To make $1,000 net (after taxes) you would probably have to work 170 hours

Here is how those 170 hours break down:

- 170 hours divided by 15 weeks in the semester would be more than 11 hours per week
- That 11 hours per week is the equivalent of almost 2 hours a day
- You also have to consider the time spent traveling to the job

Instead of spending almost two hours a day, every day, just to have $1,000 at the end of the semester, you should try to borrow that money. It can be repaid, with a low interest rate, after you have graduated. (Whichever family member lends the money should be kind enough not to charge interest while you are still in school).

If your parents loaned you $1,000 each semester, you would owe them $8,000 when you graduate. This would be in addition to any student loans owed to banks or other financial institutions.

Here is the key issue: If you agreed to spend those additional *two hours* each day doing something productive and worthwhile that will help you get more out of your college years and prepare you better for a career, you and your parents should make this deal.

Obviously, some families already give their children all they can afford and the additional $1,000 a semester would be a hardship. But it is important to recognize how many hours it takes you to earn what is a relatively small amount of money, and how those hours could be spent doing something that makes better use of your time.

The loan terms should be in writing. You and your parents should sign the document, and you should take seriously the obligation to repay the money. Remember, you will be an undergraduate one time in your life. You will be working for the next half-century or more. If they can afford it, your parents should help you get the full benefit of the college experience by lending you money beyond what they would normally give you for tuition and expenses.

The Extra Semester

Even if your parents lend you the additional money as described above, they should consider letting you take more than four years to graduate and helping you the best they can during that extra semester.

Your parents may resist this advice because they believe they are giving you a taste of the real world by insisting that you maintain a full course schedule and graduate on time. "I did it, so you can, too" a parent might say. But without realizing it, your parents may be lessening the quality of your academic experience. Unless you have been wasting time and are unmotivated about school, your parents should be flexible about when you graduate.

It is often hard to get into classes

Parents may not understand how many factors can keep you from completing all requirements within the four years. For example, it is often difficult to get into required classes during the semester in which it is best to take them. Those classes (especially if they are in different departments) may be offered at the same time, so you can only take one of them each semester. In addition, classes in your major may be full and thus you may have to wait another semester before taking them.

Universities are also under intense budget pressure. They admit large numbers of freshmen and transfer students because of the increased tuition that they bring. However, because resources are tight at many universities, there is often a bottleneck of students waiting to get into their major courses because there are too few professors and facilities such as computers or labs. Thus, students who were admitted with the idea that they would make it through college in four years may find that the lack of space in classes makes that impossible. (See Jeffrey Selingo, "Colleges and Lawmakers Push Students to Graduate in 4 years," *Chronicle of Higher Education*, November 9, 2001, p. A22).

Classes that are especially important

If you are pursuing a major that leads to a competitive job environment or one that requires you to develop specialized skills, you should consider taking an extra semester to graduate. With the extra semester, you can then take fewer credits during your final year or so. That gives you more time to spend on classes directly related to your career. You should consider doing this even if you are not working while in school.

As explained before, you will likely take only a handful of classes that help you develop job-related skills. You need to devote a substantial amount of your time and energy to each of those classes. If you are taking a full load and constantly rushing off to your job or have time-consuming classes, you will not be getting as much as you should out of those courses.

If you take a reduced load, you are likely to have 12 credits instead of 15 if your university is on a semester system. That probably means you cannot drop a class without becoming a part-time student.

Balancing "Liberal Arts" Courses with "Career" Classes

I explained in a previous chapter that it can be difficult to get into "life-enriching" classes because the students who are majoring in those subjects may have priority when it comes to registering for them. Although you may have a tough time getting into those courses, it does not mean they are unimportant.

Students who are ambitious may want to take only those classes that directly advance their career prospects. If you are a computer science major, you may not see the need for taking any writing classes other than those required by the university. Or, if you are a biology major interested in a career in that field, you may think it is a waste of time to study American history.

Unfortunately, many students and parents see college these days as nothing more than a way to prepare for a career. Some students thus believe anything not directly related to their major and career is an unnecessary digression from what they consider to be their primary reason for being at a university.

If you are helping to pay for school by working and you are an accounting major, for example, how do you or your parents justify the cost (if you have to pay for the additional credits) and time you would spend on a course on modern American art?

One way to look at it is to recognize that you will probably never have the chance to take a class like that again, especially one with a knowledgeable and experienced teacher. Also, during your working life over the next 50 years, you will earn enough so that the money spent for the art class will eventually seem like a small amount.

Another way to think about it is that college is a time to try new things. Take courses in subjects you think will enrich your life. Seek out professors and other people on campus who have done interesting things. Go to social events and meet people with a variety of backgrounds. All those experiences will make you a more well-rounded person.

You should take the right classes to prepare for the career you have planned, but you should also take classes in history, English, science, art, music, and other subjects that will make a difference in your life. A single piece of music played by a teacher in a music class, a novel assigned by an English professor, or a painting shown to you by an art teacher could inspire you to learn more. Some of those works of music, literature or art may stimulate an interest in those subjects that lasts a lifetime. Your parents should support the decision to take such "non-career" courses.

Outside Activities

A recent book by a Harvard professor who asked students about their college experience clearly demonstrates that those who participate in meaningful extra-curricular activities find their college years more fulfilling and enjoyable than those who do not. (Richard J. Light, *Making the Most of College: Students Speak Their Minds,* Harvard University Press, 2001). Because much of the learning you will do at a university will take place outside of the classroom, you should consider participation to be very important.

You could be involved in an almost endless number of outside activities: Fraternities and sororities that provide an opportunity to plan charitable events; organizations that are recognized by the student government and receive funding; student government itself; the campus newspaper, the radio and TV station and yearbook; and clubs dealing with a variety of interests.

Try new things. This may be the only time in your life you'll have this chance. Once you are working full-time, it will be much harder to get involved in so many interesting activities. This experience will not only help you in many different ways by exposing you to new people, new ideas, and new situations, it may also help with your career.

If you were an employer, would you want to hire someone who spent his or her college years doing nothing but going to classes and studying? You would probably think that such a prospective employee was not a very interesting person.

One of the best things about being in college is that successful people from the outside world regularly come to campus to talk to students. Don't miss the opportunity to hear some of those people. Many times, the speaker will not only make a public address, but will also meet students in small groups. Take advantage of this. You never know when someone will say something that will have a profound effect on you. You may also make an important contact for your career.

A Cautionary Note

If you take a reduced course load for some of the reasons that I discuss here, you may have to stick with your schedule even if you want to drop a class. At many universities, you will be considered a part-time student if you take below 12 credits in a semester.

That can have serious consequences. For example, you may be covered by your parents' health and car insurance. They need to check their policies or with their agent to see if the coverage continues even when you are going to school part-time. Many policies insure children only when they are full-time students.

If you are receiving financial aid, and your aid is dependent on your full-time status, you run the risk of losing that aid if you go part-time. You should check in advance with the financial aid office to see what rules apply.

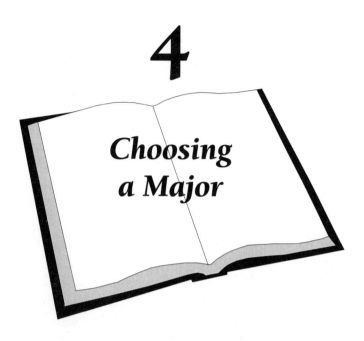

4

Choosing a Major

Summary: This chapter suggests some factors to consider when choosing a major.

Why It Matters: Few decisions are more important than your selection of a major. It will affect your college experience and your career.

Choosing a major is one of the most important decisions you will make in your life. It will have a profound impact on your experience as an undergraduate and may determine what kind of career you have. The decision as to which major is right for you will likely affect the rest of your life. Yet some students choose a major without sufficient information, and some choose one for the wrong reason and later regret it.

You may be fortunate enough to know even before the first day of classes what you want to major in and what kind of career you want. Knowing in advance what you want to do with your life is usually a good thing because you can plan ahead. But you must make sure that your career aspirations are realistic and that you have chosen the major that will best prepare you for that career.

Before choosing a major, you should do some research or at least talk to a few people who can give you good ideas before you make this important decision.

What Comes First: Career or Major?

Many students believe they know what they want to do for a living. An undergraduate major may be identified with that career, or several different majors could lead to a successful career in that field.

For example, students who are interested in going to law school can major in almost any undergraduate program. Probably most undergraduates interested in a legal career study political science or one of the other social sciences, but law schools admit students who majored in chemistry or biology or one of the other hard sciences, or in humanities such as English and history. Law schools and employers who hire lawyers appreciate a diverse background.

If, on the other hand, you are interested in a career in geology, you are almost certainly going to be a geology major. You will take courses in related fields, but you will concentrate your studies in the geology department.

One question you have to face is this: Do you select a career first, then find a major that leads to that career, or do you choose a major and once you are studying that field, eventually decide what kind of job you are interested in?

Students today have a tendency to focus so intensely on a career that they sometimes forget that a college education is supposed to give them the chance to be broadly educated without necessarily preparing them for a specific job. Many liberal arts universities offer excellent programs that introduce students to the great works of literature, expose them to scientific knowledge, and inform them of important historical events, all without teaching them "hands-on" skills that lead to one career. The idea is that broadly educated graduates will be prepared to do many different tasks, and they will learn specific job skills after leaving college.

What comes first doesn't matter that much

Whether you think about a career first then choose the appropriate major, or you decide on your major without having clear career plans, may not matter that much. The reason is that during the time you are in college, you will be exposed to a variety of courses, people, and ideas, any one of which can affect your career plans. You may change your mind several times about what interests you and what kind of job you want after college.

For example, you may have decided well before college that you want to be a physician. But after taking biology and chemistry, you may conclude that a pre-med major is not for you. After a semester or two during which time you didn't know what you were going to do with yourself after college, you may have a class with an English literature professor who excites and inspires you. You don't know specifically what career it might lead to, but you know now that you want to major in English.

Or the reverse may happen. You enter a major because you think it will help you prepare for a certain job. But as you study more in that area, you realize that although this is the right major for you, the job you thought you wanted to pursue is not what you had expected. So you stay in that field, but you know you'll be working at something other than that after college.

In some respects, it may be better not to have definite plans about what you want to do because you won't be as open to new ideas and experiences. Especially if the field you want to enter is highly competitive, you need to be willing to consider alternative careers.

Be flexible about your career plans as you pursue a major

I teach in a program that has students majoring in broadcast journalism. Although the electronic media field has many different jobs, 80 percent or more of the students have one career in mind when they enter that major: They want to be television news anchors.

Unfortunately, that is one of the most competitive positions of any industry and very few of the students entering our program will earn a living that way. However, there are many other important jobs in the broadcasting business. For example, a serious shortage of newscast producers exists at TV stations. News directors aggressively recruit students who have experience producing newscasts in their TV news classes and who work with producers during their internships. Unlike their counterparts who want to be on-air reporters or anchors, producers can start in a much larger television market and for a larger salary.

Preparing for a career as a newscast producer as opposed to a TV anchor would probably lead a student to take different courses, apply for different kinds of internships, undertake different tasks when working on a student-produced TV newscast, and do other things differently.

The problem is that students who dream unrealistically about being a TV anchor don't usually find out until very late in their college career, and sometimes not until after they graduate, that they are not going to make it in that part of the business. It may be too late by then for them to switch their focus.

Part of the reason students don't know about their career prospects is because it is difficult for professors to be fully candid with them. When talking with students about their career aspirations, professors have to find the right balance between encouraging them to pursue their dreams and telling them realistically about their chances for a successful career.

Parents may wonder whether professors are doing their children a disservice by not being honest with them early on so they can adjust their college curriculum and career plans to reflect the more realistic assessment of their prospects for finding work.

Professors, however, have to be careful about saying discouraging things to students. Students usually take very seriously any comments their professors make about their ability and self-worth. Teachers can easily say something that is hurtful to students and undermines their confidence when they intended only to help with candid career advice. Also, professors can be wrong about which students are going to be successful in their chosen field.

You need to be flexible about your career plans. You may change your mind as you continue to learn more. The job market may be different when you graduate from what it was when you started college four years earlier. Changes in technology or the health of the economy may affect what opportunities are available.

You should also remember that a liberal arts education, if it includes the development of oral and written skills, will prepare you for many different careers. You don't have to decide what you want to do for the rest of your life the minute you start college.

Be realistic

Some students are very accomplished at some skill that could lead to a successful career. For example, student athletes may excel at their sport and have a good chance of making it to the professional ranks.

However, if you are in that situation, you need to keep in mind just how competitive those opportunities are. You may be an outstanding athlete in college but still not be good enough to earn a living at your sport. Also, you could be injured at any time.

As you make your way through college, consider what you would do if you could not have the professional athletic career you had counted on. Choose a major carefully and get the most out of your courses because they may be important to your work later on.

Internships

You will be better prepared for many careers if you do an internship while you are in college. Internships can be important for a number of reasons:

- You may acquire skills that you cannot learn in your classes.
- You may be hired where you interned because your supervisor knows you and your work.
- You may get a better sense of what that career would really be like.

When preparing for an internship, here are some issues to consider:

- Some university departments require an internship so you should plan ahead.
- In many programs you must complete certain courses before you are eligible for an internship.
- Some departments will allow you to do only *one* internship for credit your entire college career. (You may be able to do additional internships that are noted on your transcript, but they may not count toward the credits you need to graduate).

- Some internships pay an hourly salary but many do not. If the internship will be beneficial, you should do it even if it does not pay.
- Whenever you do an internship for which you are getting credit, you have to pay tuition. Some students don't realize, for example, that if they do an internship during the summer, they have to register and pay for those credits. Whether the internship pays a salary doesn't affect this.

Your department or college is likely to have an internship director. Check with that person well in advance of the time you plan to do an internship to learn the requirements and what opportunities are available.

Some companies and organizations get a lot of applications from students interested in internships. Find out what they look for. If possible, try to talk to someone in person at the place where you would like to do an internship. Then, when your letter and resume arrive, you will not be just another name on a piece of paper, and you may have an advantage over other applicants.

> **Many students get jobs
> as a result of their internships.**

*Double-majoring
or "minoring"*

Some students major in two programs on campus. If they complete all the requirements, the double-major is reflected on their transcript and diploma.

If you want to complete two majors because you are getting a lot out of the courses, then you should pursue a double-major. If, however, you are doing it because you

believe it will make a difference to an employer, it is probably not worth it.

It is very hard to complete requirements for two majors
within four years. You may have to stay an extra semester to
finish up the additional courses in that major. That is probably not a good reason to stay an extra semester.

This is not inconsistent with what was said a few chapters
ago about staying an extra semester so you can get more out
of your courses. Staying longer just so you can say you double-majored isn't itself worth the extra time.

If you want to take most of the important classes in the
second department, you may be able to do it as a "minor" and
not need to complete all of the requirements. Check with
your adviser if you are interested in pursuing this.

Explaining your major or minor to a prospective employer

When you apply for a job, you will write a cover letter to
go with your resume. (You cannot send just a resume. You always need to include a letter).

In that letter, you can describe your program or the
courses you have completed. For example, if you were an
English major who also took a lot of computer science
classes, you can explain that in the letter. You do not have to
formally complete a double-major or minor in that second
field to show you benefited from that coursework. Most of the
time, prospective employers are interested in the courses you
took and what you learned, not whether you completed
enough credits so your transcript says you "double-majored"
or "minored" in a particular subject.

**Don't take courses just to complete
a second major or a minor. Take courses
if they are right for you and your career.**

Whose Major Is It:
Yours or Your Parents?

Parents influence their children's choice of college majors in both direct and indirect ways. If one of your parents is a teacher, you may be inclined to consider that profession if your parent's experience overall has been positive, without your parent ever saying that it is something you should do. Just growing up in such an environment may lead you to think about a teaching career.

Some parents, of course, are much more direct in trying to influence their child's career decisions. They make it clear, over a period of years, which professions they think are worthwhile and which ones are not. Sometimes they have such strong feelings that they will agree to pay for college only if their children consider certain majors.

Some parents, as well-meaning as they are, want their children to major in a field that leads to a career that they would have liked to pursue if they had the chance to go to college and start over again. It is probably a natural instinct to want a child to succeed in a field that they would have liked to enter.

Professors encounter some of these problems from time to time. Students whom I advise or get to know in my classes sometimes confide that their parents do not want them to be a journalist. They don't see it as an important calling, and they may have a relatively low opinion of journalists and the work they do. They may believe that journalists are unprincipled and insensitive about the potential damage they do to peoples' reputations and privacy. The situation gets worse when parents find out about the low entry-level salaries that journalists earn. On a few occasions, students have told me that their decision to major in journalism was such a sensitive subject back home, they were unable to talk with their parents about their college experience without it turning into another argument over their career plans.

Some students are under a lot of pressure to major in something that will teach job-related skills. Parents may believe that if their children major in English or American history or art, they will not be able to find work related to that major and thus their college education will have been "wasted." Instead, parents might argue that the student should major in accounting, business, or computer science, or something that will lead to a specific line of work.

When you are 18 or 19 and don't want to displease or disappoint your parents, it is hard to choose a major you know they will not like. If you are unsure what you want to do for a career, the decision may be especially difficult.

Many parents, of course, tell their children to major in anything that excites them regardless of whether it leads to a career or whether it is a major of which they approve.

You need to remember that this is your college education, not your parents'. Even if they are paying for it, they cannot tell you what is the right major for you. You need to come to that conclusion yourself. Your parents can strongly recommend that your career aspirations be realistic and that the major you choose be the appropriate one, and they can insist that you gather enough information to make a rational decision. But when it comes to making the choice of which major is right, the decision is yours. You, not your parents, will have to live with the consequences of that decision.

Researching Majors Before Deciding

You and your parents will feel much better about your choice of a major if you have done sufficient research. You can begin by exploring what kind of careers people have in that field.

The Internet provides a lot of information about jobs that is relatively easy to find. For most professions you will be able to learn how many people work in that field, how many students graduate with degrees in that major each year, what the average salaries are, where most of the jobs are located, and other related information.

**Before declaring a major,
do your homework.**

You should also consider talking to someone who has worked in the field for a number of years, but you have to be careful not to place too much emphasis on the comments of any one person. If you are considering a teaching career and a veteran teacher tells you that it is a miserable way to make a living and that he or she would have done something else if given the chance, you should not immediately change your plans. Talk to others. Read what people have written about working in that field.

Talk to professors

Professors are a good source of information about majors and careers. But you should not rely too much on the comments of any one professor. You have to consider the professor's background and experience. The professor may have worked for a business or for an organization that is different from what you are interested in. Or perhaps the professor's experience in that field was not positive and therefore the professor may be biased about the value of such a career.

The best advice will come from professors who have not only been teaching for a while but who keep in touch with graduates. Professors who do that conscientiously will be able to tell you a lot about what kinds of jobs graduates are getting, what the pay is likely to be, what opportunities there are for advancement, and whether the courses graduates took prepared them for the work they are doing.

Alumni information

Ask a professor or the alumni staff person in the department for names of graduates who are working in the profession. When you contact them, you should probably do so by phone. They can tell you more on the phone in a shorter period of time than they can by e-mail. More importantly, they are likely to speak more candidly on the phone where there is no permanent record of the conversation.

Even if people are busy, they are likely to take a few minutes to talk to you on the phone about your career aspirations. If nothing else, they may recommend another person or a source of information you can consult. People often feel affection for the college where they graduated. If you call from that college to say you soon will be choosing a major and are thinking ahead to what jobs may be available, most alumni will give you at least some advice.

Site visits

You should consider visiting a company or organization where people have the kinds of careers you may want to pursue. Although a personal visit takes more time than a phone call, a surprising number of successful and busy people will agree to meet a student in person and show them around the place where they work. They know that choosing a major is a very important decision for you. If you are assertive about this, you may be surprised at how much you can find out about the profession and the major in a short period of time.

Major requirements

Before deciding on a major, learn what courses are required. Begin by reading the university bulletin. Most departments also publish their own materials that explain the major requirements in detail and discuss the kinds of jobs their graduates pursue.

Many university departments have Web sites that also provide some of this information, but you have to check it carefully. Department Web sites are often out of date. Some have not been revised in several years. Professors who are listed in the Web site as being on the faculty are long gone, while newer professors may not have been added. The course requirements and prerequisites may also have been changed without the department Web site being updated.

If you are unsure about the requirements as described in the bulletin or the Web site, ask an adviser or professor in the department before you decide on a major. Because of the importance of this decision, you must have complete information and should not be confused about what will be expected of you once you are in the program.

As explained before, you may have to go through an application process to be accepted to that major. Check out in advance what is required for admission to the major and then realistically assess your chances. Sometimes you cannot submit an application for admission until your junior year. It may be difficult to find another major and meet all of its requirements and still graduate on time if your first choice doesn't work out.

Changing Majors

Many students, it seems, switch majors during their college careers. Depending on how closely related your old and new majors are, you may have to spend one or more semesters beyond the four years in order to complete all the requirements for the degree.

Although not graduating in four years can have financial ramifications and upset your parents, you are better off going an extra semester or two than being in the wrong major. If you are in a major that you do not find interesting or stimulating and will lead to a career you don't want, you may spend much of your working life regretting that you didn't major in something else. Changing majors is a serious matter that can cause substantial disruption in your progress toward a degree, but if the new major is really what you want to do, you should work it out so you can stay in school long enough to finish.

This is a time when you especially need good academic advice. Find a knowledgeable and patient adviser in the new department and explain the situation. See what courses you will need to take and when they will be available in order to maintain a reasonable pace toward graduation.

You should switch majors only for good reasons. Do not change your major because you got a "C" in a course, or you didn't like a professor. If, after taking a number of classes, you are thoroughly convinced that you are not interested in the substantive material you are learning, you could be in the wrong major. But it may be a serious mistake to abandon a major just because you didn't like one class.

Salary Prospects

Some students, with the encouragement of their parents, choose majors and careers based on how much money they are likely to make after graduating. Jobs in business, accounting, engineering, and computer science have a tendency to pay much more than positions filled by sociology and English majors.

You obviously have to make a decent salary to be happy and to be able to enjoy your career and life, but you need to think about whether you are going into a line of work that doesn't really interest you because you think you can make a fair amount of money quickly.

After four or five years of going to classes, interacting with classmates, professors, and friends, and going to athletic events and parties, you will be in for quite a change when you start to work.

Think about how much of your life you will spend at your job. You will likely be in the office at 8 or 9 a.m. or earlier and have to be alert and enthusiastic. Many people work incredibly long hours, and often under stressful conditions. You will soon discover that you don't have much free time. On many days, by the time you get home, you will be tired and not feel like going out. You may have to do work at home that you didn't finish during the day.

The weekends will go by quickly. You will probably run errands and do a lot of chores that have to be done that you didn't have time for during the week. All of a sudden it is Sunday night, and you have to be in bed so you can get to the office early on Monday.

You will also likely face financial pressures. You may be paying your own rent, insurance bills, and car payments for the first time. If you are also paying back student loans, your salary may be stretched thin.

As a student, you may have enjoyed having summers off, three weeks for holidays between semesters, and a week for spring break. When you are working, you may get two weeks of vacation a year and a few personal days.

What all this means is that you may have a tough time adjusting to the working world after being in college for four years or more. When you consider a major and what career to pursue, think about how much of your life will be spent at the job. Think about whether you will be happier doing what you really wanted and earning $25,000 a year, or working at a job that you may not like very much and earning $45,000. That's a lot of difference in salary and if you have student loans to pay, you may not have any choice but to take the less enjoyable job.

There are no easy answers to this, and you will have to weigh a lot of factors when making this decision. But you almost always have to choose a major before you understand what it is like to work full-time at a job you don't care for. By the time you realize you are not happy, you may have a hard time changing careers.

You can increase the chances that you will choose the right major by talking to people who work in the field, asking questions of your professors, and doing enough research so you can make an informed judgment.

Part II

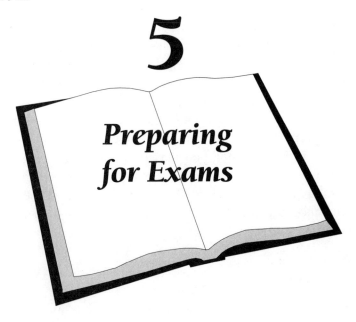

5
Preparing for Exams

Summary: This chapter discusses how to take notes, prepare for exams and learn from your classes.

Why It Matters: *Getting good grades and getting the most out of your courses are not the same, but you need to keep both in mind if college is to be meaningful for you.*

Your first college classes can be intimidating. You don't know how hard it will be to understand the substantive material, how well your professor will convey the information and explain the course requirements, and how much of your time the work will take.

If the course is not in your major, and you believe it is a subject that you are not interested in, you may be thinking only about how to get through the class with a decent grade. But that is not the way to approach college. Besides concentrating on the course material and the exams and papers, you also have to think about what the class will mean to you long after it is over. If you don't view college from that perspective, you will not be getting all that you should from the experience.

There is obviously no magical formula that you can use to do well in your classes. One factor in your success may be how prepared you are for the course. If you took related classes in high school, you may have a stronger foundation from which to approach the new material. Another important factor is whether you think the subjects covered in the course are important and interesting. You are likely to do better in a class you find stimulating.

Lectures and Class Participation

For reasons that are partly historical and partly financial, most classes have a "lecture" format. If professors and students lived in an ideal world, classes would not be taught this way. Everyone recognizes that this is not the most effective way to learn. A professor stands at the front of the room, sometimes with a computer screen, overhead or blackboard, and "lectures" to the students. The students, who are usually passive for almost the entire class period, dutifully take notes. They occasionally ask questions or make comments, but the professor usually does almost all the talking. It is easy for students to feel "uninvolved" in the class when they do little more than listen to the professor and take notes.

From time to time during the semester, you will have exams. Many times, the tests ask you to recall facts that you learned through the textbook or lecture, but they don't usually give you the chance to demonstrate that you have thought about the issues raised in the class. That is unfortunate because it is that *thinking* process—especially when you are able to discover things on you own—that stays with you far beyond the college years.

Why it is important to participate in class

Generally, the larger the class, the less time that can be spent listening to students discuss issues during the class period. If there are a hundred students, and the class meets for three 50-minute periods a week, the professor can't allow very many students to talk in class or else there won't be enough time to cover the course material. A few can ask questions, but professors will often go an entire semester without hearing from most of the students.

Sometimes smaller discussion sections meet once a week and allow you the chance to talk about issues raised in the lectures and textbook. But some universities do not schedule discussion groups unless the class is very large.

Although it would obviously be better if every student had the opportunity to talk, it is worthwhile to hear from even a few students as the class tries to understand new concepts. When students speak in class, it often gives professors feedback about how well they understand the material. If there is confusion, the professor can explain it again in a different way.

By participating in class discussion, you will feel more engaged in the course.

For learning to take place, students must be interested in the class and the course material. By hearing from your classmates and contributing to classroom discussion yourself, you are likely to be more engaged in the subject.

You should be assertive about talking in class. The professor will probably signal how much time he or she wants to allow for student questions and comments. Once you get a sense of that, you should volunteer comments that help you to think about what you are learning. Talking in class will help you in a number of ways:

> ➤ It forces you to *articulate* the concepts and facts that you have been reading and hearing about in the textbook and lectures. If nothing else, you will likely remember what you talked about that day, especially if you were able to put various concepts together or discover your own way of thinking about the material. If the professor asked you follow-up questions that required additional thinking, you will almost certainly remember that exchange.
>
> You may be able to absorb information by reading the textbook and listening to the lectures well enough for the exams. But that does not mean you have learned the material for the long-term or that it has stretched your mind. That requires more active involvement on your part. Passively listening to lectures for 15 weeks is often not enough engagement in the course material for it to stay with you.
>
> ➤ By articulating the concepts aloud, you must find your *own* words to describe the material the class has been studying. It is not easy to speak off the top of your head as you struggle to describe complicated concepts. You may be a little nervous depending on the number of students in the class and the demeanor of the professor.
>
> But even if your description is not sophisticated or precise, the process of explaining the issue has likely contributed to your learning. Instead of simply mimicking or memorizing what the professor said or what was

in the textbook, you had to find words to describe the concept and that required thinking about the material.

➤ Being able to analyze, interpret, evaluate and sometimes criticize facts, events and issues is an essential part of learning. When you have graduated from college, you will face difficult situations on the job and in your life. Your ability to analyze those situations and determine how best to respond may be related to how well you learned to master those skills in college, including in courses that seemed to have nothing to do with your major.

➤ You may impress the professor who will then get to know you well enough to recommend you for scholarships, graduate or professional school, or a job.

The question you do not want to ask

Most professors believe passionately in the importance of their teaching and research. They are often interested in highly specialized topics and don't understand why everyone isn't as fascinated by those subjects.

For me, the history of the First Amendment and what freedom of speech and freedom of the press mean to a democratic society are among the most important subjects I discuss with my students. I don't just want to explain how long it took for people in this country to be able to exercise First Amendment rights; I want to inspire students. I want them to recognize that as citizens, they have a responsibility to be knowledgeable about the First Amendment and to protect its freedoms.

After I make an impassioned, and I hope, eloquent presentation on this subject, I see a student's hand raised. When that student speaks, I will know that I have had an impact on their lives. From now on these students will think about the First Amendment and what it means. I am confident that they will read books about the founding of the nation and will take an interest in public affairs. I call on the student who then asks:

"Do we have to know that for the exam?"

Few things are more demoralizing to a teacher than that question. In response, I try to explain that students should be interested and excited about the subject because of its importance regardless of whether it will be on the test. I say something about college being a time to gain knowledge and experience new things and that students should not limit themselves to "learning" just what they need to for good grades.

You should be inspired by the course material and not just interested in what you need to know for the exams.

My advice is don't ask that question of your professor, at least not that way. If the subject is significant enough for the teacher to spend precious class time discussing it and to do so with enthusiasm, it probably will be on the exam. But more importantly, don't approach college with that attitude. If you do, when you are done, you will have a diploma and memories of athletic events and parties, and not much else.

Taking Notes

Because many of your classes will have a lecture format and the exams will include material that you heard in class, it is essential that you learn to take notes well. (You obviously should take notes to help you learn the material without regard to what will be on the exams, but it is difficult to do well on the tests without a good record of what was said in class). A few of these suggestions may seem obvious, but they are worth discussing because they are such an important component of success in the classroom:

Don't write down every word

You probably couldn't do this even if you wanted, but it is not necessary. By the first few class meetings, you will get a sense of what you should write down, but always keep in mind that you have to find a balance between writing and listening. It is hard to listen to what the professor is saying as you are writing notes. Finding that balance is not easy, and some professors make it unnecessarily difficult.

A good professor will make it clear to students what is important enough to be included in their notes. The professor may make this explicit by saying, "This is important, you should write this down." Sometimes they do so more subtly, but you can often tell from the way professors have written the concepts on the blackboard or by the way they discuss them that they are something important.

Some professors, however, make it hard for you to know what is significant enough to write in your notes. They don't seem to emphasize any part of the material. Instead, they present all the facts and concepts the same way and don't provide clues that something is particularly important.

Students dislike that. If a professor conducts class that way, you will feel lost and may not do very well on the exams because you won't know what parts of the textbook or lectures you need to study closely.

Here are some things you should listen for and try to write down during the lectures:

- definitions
- basic principles
- differing positions on an issue
- any timeline or series of dates
- material the professor highlights by
  —writing on the board
  —including on the overhead
  —presenting in a visual medium such as PowerPoint.

You should also learn to recognize and write down key phrases, use abbreviations, and develop your own symbols for frequently used names or phrases.

Reviewing your notes

Students sometimes take notes in class and look at them a month or two later just before an exam. That is not a good way to prepare for exams and get the most out of your classes. Here is how you should make use of your notes:

➤ After class or later that day, take a few minutes to review your notes. This serves two important purposes. First, it allows you to expand your notes, fill in missing items and clear up material you wrote too hurriedly to make sense of later. And second, reviewing your notes and the related material in the textbook for even 15 minutes will help you remember what's important for the next class and for the exam.

➤ Review your notes throughout the semester. You may have written down something the professor said in class, but later when you look at your notes, you don't understand it. If you wait until just before the exam to ask the professor to clarify, it may be too late because there are no more class periods before the test. Look at your notes on a regular basis so you can ask the professor to explain confusing concepts, then update your notes so it will be clear when you study for the test.

Instead of waiting until a day or two before the exam to go over material you may not have looked at for weeks, it is much better to review regularly. Before beginning a reading assignment and before the next lecture, skim the material in the textbook that you previously read and underlined or highlighted. Look over your notes from the previous lecture and think about the material that was presented during that class period.

One reason so few students do this is that they worry that they will duplicate the studying they have to do in the days leading up to the exam. Students sometimes believe that they have to review the material just before the exam in order to remember enough of it to do well.

What some students don't think about is that if they review their notes and the textbook *throughout* the semester, they will be able to accomplish much more when they study for the exam. Instead of the material being a distant memory because it was presented a month or two ago, you will be more familiar with it, and you won't have to spend time the night before "re-learning" it. That will give you more time to concentrate on areas you didn't understand.

Students do not all learn the same way. Some, for example, have disabilities that affect how they are able to absorb information in lectures and prepare for exams. The discussion in this section will obviously not apply the same to all students.

Not everything will be tested

Some students want to study only what they believe will be on the exams, but there is a good reason not to approach your classes that way. A relatively small percentage of the material presented in class and in the textbook will be on the exams. If you confine yourself to what will be tested, you will be learning only a small portion of the material presented in the classroom and textbook. Of course, you don't always know exactly what will be asked, so you may study material beyond what is on the exams, but the lesson is still the same. You should not try to guess what will be on the tests, then study only the bare minimum you need to get a decent grade.

Assume for a moment that you will read all of a 500-page textbook during the semester. Here is how the number of words in the book will compare to what you hear in class and what will be on the exam:

- If each page of the textbook has 400 words, you will have read 200,000 words in the book during the semester. (It is obviously important concepts, not words, that matter. But a word count is used here to illustrate the point).
- You will also attend about 30 lectures a semester (many classes meet twice a week for 75 minutes each).
- That means you will be in class for about 37 hours, during which the professor will do most of the talking.

That adds up to a lot of written and spoken words.

Now think about how many of those words will be tested. Only a small percentage can be on the exam. Here's why:

> If there is one midterm (usually one 75-minute class period) and a two-hour final, you will have a little more than three hours during the entire semester to show what you learned from reading 200,000 words and from listening to 37 hours of lectures.

That is why it is so important for professors to find the right balance between telling you what you need to know for the exam and helping you discover what is important on your own.

Even if you attend all the lectures, pay close attention and believe you have a good sense of what are the most significant concepts, professors may not do their part. Sometimes teachers make it clear in class which concepts and issues are the most important, and students dutifully take notes on that material. But when you take the first exam, you discover that the professor has asked very little about what you and your classmates were convinced were the "major" concepts. Instead, you were asked a lot of questions about issues that may have been barely mentioned in class or were buried within the text of the book.

Students understandably think this is unfair and is a sign of poor teaching. But again, from the professor's perspective, writing exams that are fair *and* challenging is very difficult to do. If students know they will be tested only on the lectures in class, they will barely read the textbook. If the professor tells them what to study for the exam, they may ignore what they consider to be the extraneous portions of the lectures and book and will thus learn less during the semester than they would otherwise.

No one lectures and prepares exams in exactly the same way. There are always going to be times when professors believe they have prepared students for a challenging exam, one that will reward those who study the most, only to find later that they didn't cover some of the material thoroughly enough for students to do well. For the professor, it is hard to know if the students who did poorly did not study for the exam, or if they prepared conscientiously but just didn't know what to expect.

One other thing is worth mentioning. Professors should think about how to test students fairly throughout the semester. But professors have a tendency to concentrate on the material they are presenting and are not necessarily thinking all the time about the exams. Professors don't want the "test" to determine the content of the course and how it is taught. They want to present the subject in the most exciting way possible and then figure out the best method for determining who studied hard.

Don't tape record the lectures

With all the material that a professor presents, sometimes at a very fast pace, you may be tempted to record the lectures so you can play them back. By starting and stopping the tape, you can take notes at your own pace.

You should probably not do this for two reasons: It takes too long to listen to the tapes, and you will not likely take notes during the lecture if you know there is a tape recording of it you can listen to later.

It takes much less time to review notes than to listen to a complete tape. If you have taken notes well, you will have a good record of the most important material. You would have to listen to the entire tape to know whether you have recognized the most important aspects of the lecture and that can take time away from learning the major concepts in the class and reading the textbook.

You may also be missing important things from the live lecture. If you know you are taping it, you may not take notes during class time. Simply by taking notes you are more engaged in the learning process. Most teachers would say that a student who writes something down is more likely to remember the material than a student who didn't, even if the student who took notes never reviews the material. It is the act of putting the words on paper that helps students to remember and learn.

If you are recording the lecture, you may not feel the need to pay close attention to what the teacher is discussing because you assume you will get to it later. Moreover, if the professor uses the blackboard or overhead to illustrate something, you will not be able to duplicate that when listening after class to the taped lecture.

It is important to mention, however, that some students have a difficult time taking notes. If you are one of those students, you should ask the professor if it is all right to record the lectures.

Relying on others' notes
when you miss class

In a semester in which you have four or five classes stretching over a 15-week period, it is likely that you will miss some class periods. You may be tempted to get the notes from a friend or someone who is sitting near you in the class. That may not be a good idea.

First, their notes may be hard to decipher. Everyone takes notes differently and material that you would have considered important enough to write down may not have seemed that way to the person whose notes you are borrowing.

Second, their notes may be incomplete but because you weren't at the lecture, you would probably have no way of knowing that. If the student skipped some important issues, he or she would not likely indicate that in the notes. It would be the same if the student stopped taking notes for the last 15 minutes of the class out of fatigue or boredom.

Third, the notes could be wrong. The student whose notes you are borrowing may have been confused or written down facts or names incorrectly. But it is not always obvious just from looking at the notes that something is inaccurate.

If you miss class, be sure you get access to complete and accurate lecture notes.

The best way to handle this situation, although it can be a bit delicate, is to tell the professor that you missed class and would like to see the notes of someone the professor recommends. Except in very large classes, professors usually know by the first few weeks of the semester which students appear to be taking thorough notes. See if the professor will ask one of those students to share notes with you.

You may think that the easiest thing to do is to ask the professor for his or her notes. But that is often not a good solution.

As with many professors, I do not lecture from detailed notes but instead use either a brief outline, or sometimes if I am especially familiar with the material, no notes at all. From time to time, just before class starts, I look at the notes of a few students to see what material they considered important enough to write down from the past few classes. Sometimes I look at their notes to see what I said and where I left off.

Professors will usually agree to meet with students who have missed class, but they often prefer that the student get the notes from a classmate. The students may have a more detailed recollection of what was said in class than the professor because they were taking notes and the professor has other classes. Also, professors do not always have enough time to summarize their lectures in their office for students who have missed class. If there are a large number of students in the class, this can be very time-consuming. If there are teaching assistants, they may be able to perform this function. If you have questions after you have read the notes of a classmate, you should talk to the professor.

How Professors View Exams

Before you study for an exam, it is helpful to know what the professor may be thinking as he or she prepares a test. Several issues will play an important role in how a professor approaches exams.

How long will it take to grade?

This may seem like an unusual factor in determining the format of an exam, but it is one of the first things many professors think about when preparing a test. Writing and grading exams can take a lot of time. Two principles generally hold true for exams, and you can be sure that your professor will have thought about these issues:

> • The more comprehensive an exam, the longer it will take to grade.
> • By choosing a certain format, professors can save time in the preparation or the grading of exams, but not both.

Starting with the first principle, for many classes, it would be best to test the students with a combination of formats. For example, in a political science class, students should answer short answer, fill-in-the-blank, and multiple-choice questions that test specific facts and concepts. If the course is about the American presidency, a short-answer or multiple-choice question may ask what year a president was elected.

But professors want to know that you have learned more about a president's administration than the names of some cabinet members and the year the president took office. They want to know that you have thought about the impact of various policy decisions undertaken during that presidency and that you have come to your own conclusions about whether they reflected positively on the administration and were good for the country. That cannot be tested in a short-answer exam, but instead requires you to write an essay.

An exam that has nothing but short answer questions can be graded very quickly. If the class is large, with hundreds of students, professors can use grade sheets on which students fill in a "bubble," as when you take standardized tests, and the grading can be done by a computer. It takes very little time to do the grading that way.

But if a professor assigns essays, it will take days or even several weeks to grade them. Part of the reason is that students' handwriting is usually poor when they are nervous and rushing to get as much down as they can, and it deteriorates as they get tired.

In addition, the professor and teaching assistant, if there is one, usually need to make comments on the essays. Although the professor can explain in class what some of the common problems were with the answers, that does not replace the value of making individual comments on the exam that will be useful for students to know for the next test.

Take-home exams will be written on a typewriter or computer, so the professor doesn't have to read poor handwriting. Those exams also give students more time to prepare thoughtful answers. But such tests take a lot of time to grade. In addition, there is always the possibility that the student received help from someone in preparing the take-home essay, something the professor is not likely to know.

Most professors dislike grading exams

Not only does grading essays take a while, it is one of the least enjoyable things that professors do. Teachers must decipher student handwriting and read answers to the same essay questions over and over. If the professor has made the exam too long, students will be rushing to get down as many words as they can because they don't have enough time and thus the student handwriting may be more difficult to read. Professors may have a hard time focusing on the essays and making helpful comments when there are many exams to grade.

Thus, professors often give short answer tests knowing that they will not measure a student's understanding of many of the important issues in the class but will instead reward students for remembering certain facts. Although professors hate to sacrifice the deeper understanding that students would demonstrate on an essay exam, they give a much less comprehensive short answer exam because it takes less time to grade.

Writing the exam

The second principle is the relationship between preparing and grading exams.

It usually takes a lot longer to write a short answer, fill-in-the-blank, multiple-choice exam, than it does an essay exam. With short answer tests, you have to come up with a lot of good questions, perhaps 40 or 50 or more, that cover important subjects in the class. The questions must be drawn from the lectures and textbook, and most importantly, must not be so "trivial" that the students would have not expected them to be on the test. Writing that many good questions cannot be done in a few hours. (Because it is so time-consuming, some professors use the same short-answer exam every semester). The payoff is that it takes almost no time to grade them.

Essay questions, on the other hand, can be written in a short period of time, but as mentioned before, take a long time to grade. Whatever time a professor has saved while preparing such an exam is lost, many times over, by how long it takes to grade the essays.

The exams are supposed to reward the students who work hard

All professors have a basic goal in mind when they prepare exams: They want the students who studied the hardest —and who made a substantial effort to not only learn the material but also to give the issues some thought—to do well. You may have figured out by now that accomplishing that goal is difficult. To accomplish this, the professor has to do all of the following things:

- Choose the right textbook
- Assign the most important sections of the textbook
- Explain the material from the book in the lectures
- Present material in the lectures that supplements the textbook
- Select the best format for the exam
- Ask the questions that can be answered by students who have attended class regularly, taken good notes, and studied hard

If any one of these steps is not done well, the exams are not likely to test fairly the material in the course. Even experienced teachers find this to be difficult.

Interestingly, professors rarely get advice on how to prepare exams. They can't ask their students in advance what questions would test the material most fairly because it would be like telling them what will be on the exam. They can't talk to their colleagues about their exams because those other faculty members don't know what the professor lectured on in the class and may not know the subject well.

A professor can't even talk to students about this very easily after the exam is over. How would it sound if a professor said this to students: "For those of you who studied hard for this exam, did you think the questions were fair? If not, what questions would have been fair?" There is no way of knowing which students carefully prepared for the exam and which ones did not. Just asking the number of hours they studied doesn't help. Professors have no way of knowing who concentrated thoroughly on the material and who superficially skimmed the pages of the textbook and lectures notes for a few hours.

Over time, professors adjust questions based on how well students answer them. If many students in the class get a question wrong, the professor will either eliminate or rephrase the question or will explain the material more thoroughly in lectures. But a professor may not know for some time the best way to find out if the students have learned certain material.

How closely related should the exam be to the lectures and textbook?

When writing exams, professors have to decide how many questions should be based on the material in the lectures and how many should come from the textbook.

Let's say a professor gives three exams during the semester. On the first exam, the students find that 80 percent of the questions could have been answered just by attending lectures and taking notes, and without reading the textbook. What happens for the next exam? Students may not read the textbook carefully, or at all.

If, on the other hand, 80 percent of the questions come from the textbook, many students will stop coming to class, especially if there are hundreds of students and it is impractical for a professor to take attendance.

The exam has to be balanced in this respect so students will feel the need to both read the textbook and come to class. But then the professor faces a dilemma. Should the textbook cover subjects A, B, C, and D, and the lectures E, F, G, and H, with all eight subjects tested equally on the exam?

That won't work because in every course, the textbook introduces complex subjects that require explanation and examples in class. If students could learn the material just by reading the textbook, there would be no need for professors. Lectures need to provide context and perspective, explain difficult issues, convey to students how interesting and important the subject is, and relate the material to the professor's personal experience or research.

As the semester progresses, the professor may give clues as to whether the material from the textbook or lectures will constitute a greater part of the exam. But sometimes professors are intentionally vague about this because they don't want students to miss class or not read the textbook.

Preparing for Exams

At some point before the first test, the professor should have described the format for the exam. That is only fair and helps you to prepare. If the professor has not discussed this, you should ask. Sometimes, however, professors don't like to say much about the exact format. They worry that it will have too much of an effect on how you study. They want you to learn the material, not adopt a strategy for test-taking.

Next, you should consider how many students are in the class and whether teaching assistants are available to help with the grading. Depending on the subject being covered, once a class reaches about 40 students, a professor starts to face many hours of grading. Although you should study for the exam so you can answer both short answer and essay questions, you can assume that the larger the class, the more likely the professor will use a format that is faster to grade. If the professor in a large class has been vague about the exam format, you may be on safer ground studying for an exam that includes short-answer questions.

However, if a teaching assistant is doing the grading and he or she has only 20–30 students in the discussion section, the exam could be an essay format even though there are many students in the overall class.

Short-answer or multiple-choice exams may be harder than essay tests. In an essay exam or exams that require a few sentences of writing for some questions, you may be able to get partial credit by addressing at least some of the concepts the professor is looking for. In a short-answer test, it will most likely be all or nothing.

Depending on the subject, you may study for the two types of exams differently. With fixed answer tests, you are looking for specific issues and facts, and you can expect that even if some of them are relatively trivial, a professor will have to ask you questions from the book or lectures that yield definite answers. Essays, on the other hand, require you to study the larger concepts. You still need to know many of the basic facts because your essay will be much stronger if you include some of those, but you have to look at the "big picture" when preparing for an essay exam.

Start with your lecture notes

In preparing for the first exam in the class, review all of your lecture notes first. That will give you a good feel for the parameters of the material. At this point, don't get bogged down in too much detail. As you read through your notes, look for major concepts. What issues did the professor emphasize? Did the professor refer to a particular concept or set of facts more than once? Did the professor write a list on the blackboard or overhead that appears to be important?

Often, when a professor has taken the time to provide an actual list and has included the exact wording for the items on the list, it likely means that you will be asked about that on an exam.

Although the lecture notes, if done well, provide a good summary of the course material, you need to remember that not all of the exam questions are likely to come from the "formal" part of the lecture. Professors often digress from their notes or outline to give an example, tell an anecdote, or provide more explanation if it appears that the class is confused about something.

Sometimes professors don't remember what they said in class. So when students look at their lecture notes in preparation for the exam, they have to consider the possibility that they have a better record and recollection of what the professor said than the professor does.

Despite these potential problems, begin with your lecture notes. It is the fastest and, in many respects, the most efficient way of reviewing the course material. After you have completed a brief look at your notes, go over them again. At this point, you should read them carefully and commit to memory those subjects of the course that would likely appear on either a short-answer or essay exam, depending on which format the professor said the exam will be.

Then the textbook

After a thorough review of your notes, you need to look over the textbook. If you have underlined or highlighted your textbook carefully, you should begin with those sections. It is worth mentioning that you should bring the textbook to class every day. Many times professors will refer to something in the textbook, and that is a clue that the material from those passages may appear on the exam. If you don't have the textbook with you, you could note the page number and briefly describe the material in your class notes, then mark it later in the book. But it is better to have the textbook in class.

> **Bring your textbook to class every day so you can highlight sections of the book that the professor mentions in the lectures.**

You probably realize that hardbound textbooks have large margins so you can indicate important passages. This will save you a lot of time when you study for exams. Don't assume that the book's index will do this for you. If a professor has suggested that a subject is important, write a brief description in the margin of the textbook next to the material so you can find it easily later. If it seems especially important, you can put a "star" or some other symbol to indicate that.

If you have limited time to study for the exam, you could re-read the sections you have marked and skim other parts of the textbook. But if you have been studying throughout the semester and have followed the advice given here of regularly reviewing your lecture notes, you will not have to read again every word of the textbook chapters assigned for that exam.

What some students try, and which rarely works well, is to leave the reading of the textbook to the last minute. Students sometimes think they can read the assigned chapters the night before the exam and then do well on the test the next day because the material will be fresh in their minds.

This usually doesn't work. There is often too much material to read that way. Students would have a hard time answering essay questions requiring them to show they have thought about the issues if they read it for the first time the night before. Unless you have become interested in the course material throughout the semester, you will not likely retain much of the information even though you read it just before the exam.

Remember that each college course is supposed to have meaning for you beyond graduation day. If you do not study regularly during the semester and instead cram for exams at the last minute, you will probably not do well on tests, and you certainly won't remember much about the substantive issues in the class after you have left college.

Try never to miss the class just before an exam. Professors will often answer review questions and may provide hints as to what will be on the test.

Study groups or going it alone

Students sometimes study in groups of two, three or more. Depending on the subject of the course and how the work is divided among the group, this approach can help you prepare for exams. But all too often time is wasted because of the temptation to talk about extraneous issues and because not everyone comes to the group prepared enough to contribute much.

To make this work, students need to divide the course into subjects with each member of the group being responsible for presenting the material on that subject. The advantage is that not everyone needs to cover all the material in detail. You should be generally familiar with all the subjects, but your classmate will know more and will be able to share that increased knowledge with the group. You will do the same for your subject.

This is not cheating or inappropriate. Professors want you to learn the material. It would be great if students would not just exchange facts and specific concepts in the study groups but would also discuss the issues, which students usually have little time to do in class. Professors hope that by discussing important concepts with fellow students, you will be able to do some thinking about the subject that will make it more meaningful and interesting.

More time to complete the exam

If you have a condition that affects how you take exams, you should tell the professor in advance or contact the office on campus that helps students with disabilities. That office may give you a letter to show your professor who will then allow you additional time to take the exam or have you write it in a quieter environment.

After the Exam Has Been Graded

When a professor hands back an exam, especially if it is the first one of the semester, he or she should spend some class time talking about general problems with the answers and how students can improve. Similar problems almost always arise with many of the exams. It is worth class time to talk about those issues.

Once a professor has done so, students may feel that they were not treated equitably. They may believe that based on the professor's explanation, they should have received more credit for certain answers. They may have compared their answer to those of a classmate who received more points for what seems like a similar response.

It is not something professors want to spend much time doing, but they have to make students feel comfortable about coming to see them to look over their exams to make sure they were treated fairly.

Before going to see a professor about your exam, leave the original copy in the professor's mailbox (or give it to the professor after class), and say that you will come during his or her office hours to discuss it. If the exam has essays, the professor must have the chance to re-read them before your appointment. That will make the office visit more productive. You need to make a copy of the exam before dropping it off or giving it to the professor in case it is misplaced.

A fine line: don't try to negotiate grades

Students should go see their professors (or the teaching assistant if that is the person who did the grading) if they have questions about the way their exams were evaluated. If a professor sees that your answer or essay should have received more points, he or she will almost always change it. If the answer was graded correctly, the professor will explain to you what was wrong with it and how to prepare better for the next test.

When having this discussion with your professor, you should stick to the exam and the way it was graded. You don't want to say to a professor that you need some additional points because that will give you an "A" and your sorority or fraternity house needs that grade to have the highest GPA on campus. Or, don't argue for a higher grade because your parents will disown you if you get another "C."

Professors hear heartbreaking stories all the time. They have students who work many hours a week to help pay for school, and thus they don't have much time to study. Or the student may be a single parent, have serious health problems, or is struggling financially.

All of those problems may be real, but they have nothing to do with the answer on the exam. Out of fairness to other students and to maintain the integrity of the system, professors must confine their grading decisions to relevant issues. Do not try to negotiate grades with your professors by introducing unrelated matters. Professors often resent it and may be less likely to change the grade.

Staying in a class

I am amazed by the number of students who drop a course because they got a "C" on the first exam. I explain both before and after the exam that many students don't do that well on the first test because they may not have known what to expect, or they studied the wrong material but can see now what they need to do for the next time.

I also say to students that if their grades go up over the semester, their final grade may reflect that improvement beyond the average that the scores would yield. That means a student who gets a "C" on the first exam could get an "A" for the class if there is substantial improvement, even if the overall average at the end doesn't quite reach the "A" threshold.

Despite that, some students are so concerned about grades and so afraid they may get a "C" in the class, they drop it even after five or six weeks of the semester. They then take the class again, sometimes from the same professor, or another class that fulfills that requirement.

> ## Do not drop a class because you think you may get a "C."

Students should not do this. Grades are important, but they should not control how and what you learn in your classes. Students who drop classes because they want a higher GPA are wasting their own time and money, or their parents' money. By taking it again, they may prevent another student from being able to get into the class.

Students rarely tell professors they are planning to drop the class. They just don't show up after the exam, and it is usually weeks later before the professor is notified by the registrar's office that the student has officially left the class. In smaller classes, the professor will see that the student never returned after the first exam.

Incredibly, some students do this without seeing what their grade was on the first test. Perhaps they think they will be embarrassed when the exams are returned, although professors are careful not to reveal one student's grade to another student. Sometimes they think they did poorly when in fact their grade wasn't that bad. By the time the professor finds out the student has dropped the class, it is too late to explain to the student that he or she could have ended up with a decent grade by doing better on the next exam and should have stayed in the class.

In my many years of teaching, I have never told a student to drop a class. When students do poorly on the first test, I offer to spend time with them in my office explaining what went wrong and how to do better the next time. Almost every student, with or without a meeting, does better on the next exam.

The Parents' Role

Some parents put so much pressure on their children to get good grades that they feel they have no choice but to drop a class if they think they may get a "C." A parent of an incoming freshman told me that if his daughter ever had a semester in which she earned below a 3.0 (B) average, he and his wife would immediately stop paying for school. He said that they were providing their daughter with a "scholarship" to attend college, and according to the parents, that scholarship ends the moment she gets below a 3.0.

Although parents need to encourage their children to study hard and earn good grades, such a rigid system is not helpful to students and may, in the long run, prevent them from getting as much as they should from their college experience.

In the first few semesters, students have to take some difficult courses in math and science, and it is not unusual for someone not majoring in those subjects to get a "C" in the class. In the case of the parent mentioned above, if the daughter in her first semester gets a "C" in calculus and physics, a "B" in biology, a "B" in English, and an "A" in American government, her parents will cut her off in December because of her 2.8 average.

Such an attitude is short-sighted and potentially harmful to the student's educational experience. Over the course of four years, the student will have the chance to improve that 2.8 GPA. Many students who take difficult courses and have trouble adjusting to college life don't do that well their first semester or two even though they are genuinely trying. When students feel that kind of pressure from their parents, they will often drop classes up until the halfway point in the semester if they think they are going to get a "C" and disappoint their family. That is not the way that either parents or students should approach college.

I am not saying that parents should overlook consistently poor grades and should not take action that encourages their children to be more serious about their schoolwork. But parents need to consider the broader picture. Making their children feel so stressed about grades can lead to emotional problems and force students to choose classes based not on what they will learn, but on what grade they will get.

Don't Change Majors Based on One Exam

Not long ago I taught introduction to journalism to a class that consisted mostly of freshmen and sophomores. One of the purposes of the course, which all our "pre-majors" take, is to expose them to the parameters of the field so as they go on to other courses, they will have a better idea what is available and what they may want to do for a career.

Some students did not do well on the first exam. After the test, which was given during the fifth week of a 15-week semester, I asked the students to fill out an evaluation so they could tell me, anonymously, what they liked about the course and what changes I should consider making.

Some students said they had decided not to major in journalism. And their reason? Because they didn't do well on the first exam. Those students thought because they received, for example, a 75 on the test instead of the "B" or "A" they usually get, that they weren't capable of a successful journalism career or were no longer interested in the field. One student said coming to this conclusion was devastating, because he or she had always dreamed of being a journalist.

I was disturbed by those comments. The idea that because some students in their first journalism class ended up with a 75 instead of the 83 they would have received had they answered a few more questions correctly, and now wanted to reconsider their career plans, bothered me. It demonstrated just how much grades, as opposed to what they learn, matter to many students and their parents.

No student should change majors based on one course or one exam. Some students who took the introduction to journalism class had a better understanding of the field and decided it wasn't for them. That makes sense. But what makes no sense is the idea that whenever you run the risk of getting something other than an "A" or "B" in a class, you should switch majors to one where you would get higher grades. If students have dreamed of a certain career, they and their parents should not allow one exam or one class to deter them from pursuing it.

6

Writing Papers

Summary: This chapter discusses papers you will write for your classes and how to avoid plagiarism.

Why It Matters: Not only is writing papers important for your grades, you will need to develop research and writing skills for almost any profession you consider.

You will write research papers in many of your classes. Learning to gather information and write coherently is essential if you are going to succeed in college, and it is an important skill in almost every career. But developing writing skills is difficult and it can take years to learn to write well.

The papers you write for your classes will vary from a few pages to 30 pages or more. Some professors assign several short papers, while others ask you to write one long research paper.

Professors want students to write papers for several reasons. Research papers give you the chance to go beyond just memorizing facts or concepts for an exam. Ideally, a paper will show the professor that you not only understand the material, but that you have thought about the issues in a creative way. You need to learn how to analyze and interpret information and present it in a way that shows that you have learned something and that you are developing your writing ability.

Some Students Don't Write Very Well

If you were to ask professors what skill students lack, and which are among the most difficult to teach, most would say writing. High school teachers do the best they can under difficult circumstances, but for whatever reason, college students often do not write very well, especially in the first few years. Even some juniors and seniors who are getting good grades still cannot write a decent research paper or take-home exam, despite having written a lot of papers and exams during their years in college.

The lack of writing skills shows up in different ways. Sometimes students don't know or have forgotten basic rules of grammar. Their subjects and verbs don't agree. They use the wrong word. They don't vary their sentence structure and thus often write one short declarative sentence after another. That results in choppy, abrupt writing that doesn't flow very well and isn't easy to read.

Students often don't know where to end one paragraph and begin the next. A single paragraph can go on for one or two pages. Or they will do the reverse. Instead of writing a complete paragraph that develops the idea introduced in the first sentence, they will begin a new paragraph when they should have continued the previous one.

Students often make spelling mistakes or use the wrong form of a word. It is surprising to see how many students spell the word "receive" incorrectly; who don't know that you can't say "amount" of people; who don't use "effect" and "affect" the right way; and many other such problems. Computer spell-checking programs help, but if you use a wrong word that the computer recognizes as a real word, you may not know that you have made an error.

These are serious problems, but they are not the most troublesome. The biggest problem is that many undergraduates seem to believe that simple, straightforward, clear writing is not good writing. Somehow students have gotten the idea that research papers or take-home exams should consist of mostly complex and convoluted sentences.

It is hard to know whether this idea came from parents or teachers, or from watching thousands of hours of television before college. Many students believe they will impress someone with their writing only if they use multiple phrases or clauses and words that are found on the SAT but are rarely used in real life. The result is often awkward writing that is difficult to understand.

**Simple, straightforward,
clear writing is good writing.**

Look at these examples from a media law take-home exam. For this assignment, the student is playing the role of a judge and must decide which of the two courts' decisions is more persuasive and explain why. The student in the first example is explaining that two federal courts of appeals came to opposite conclusions on the same issue.

> "This decision places this court in a distinct minority with the First Circuit Court due [to] its ruling for the

Providence Journal of Rhode Island in 1986 which held that a contempt charge based on an unconstitutional ruling, with regards to First Amendment rights, could not be upheld in that case."

This is probably what the student meant:

"I must decide whether the ruling by the First Court of Appeals in the *Providence* case is more persuasive than the decision by the Fifth Circuit in *Dickinson*. Based on the reasons discussed below, I have come to the conclusion that the *Providence* case better protects First Amendment rights while at the same time respecting judicial authority."

Here is a section of another student's exam addressing the same topic:

"On the one hand, you have the Fifth Circuit in *Dickinson* that feels a court's authority is more powerful than a writer's amendment protection even when the court's rulings are unconstitutional."

This is probably what the student meant:

"The Fifth Court decided that it is so important that judicial orders be obeyed, even when they may be unconstitutional, that the First Amendment cannot be used to justify a decision by a journalist to defy a court order."

Any professor who assigns writing projects would be able to offer dozens of similar examples.

Professors May Not Be Able to Help Much

Many students probably believe that if they begin college with underdeveloped writing skills, their professors will work closely with them to help. That happens in a few classes, but in most cases students will be disappointed if they expect that kind of personal attention from their teachers.

Helping students with their writing takes a lot of time

Think for a moment about what is required for your writing to improve. Depending on how bad it was to begin with, a teacher would have to make detailed comments on the paper and then go over the comments with you in person. Then you would need to rewrite the paper (or at least sections of it) and make the changes the professor recommended. However, it is not enough for you simply to re-do the paper and substitute the professor's phrases. You have to understand why there was a problem in the initial paper and why the teacher's solution is a better way of doing it.

Let's say you are a student in an American history class along with 50 others. The professor or teaching assistants (if there are any) want to make comments on the 10-page research paper you handed in, but they can write only a few words in the margins and a brief note at the end.

Why? Because it takes too long to read 500 pages of material and make extensive comments on them. If there are more students in the class or the research paper is longer, it would take even more time for the professor to write detailed notes on your paper.

This situation makes it difficult for the teacher to help you with your writing. Professors usually have time to comment only on problems in the paper related to the substance of the material in the class, not on writing deficiencies. They may circle spelling errors or typos and may write the word "awkward" or "unclear" next to a sentence or paragraph, but they don't have the time to fix basic writing problems. Professors may not get the chance to talk to you about the paper and are not likely to require you to revise it.

There are some classes in English and in journalism where the emphasis is on writing, and sometimes classes are small enough that professors can work closely with you on these problems. But relatively few courses will focus on how to improve your writing ability.

Professors may not know how to help you with your writing

Professors often see essays or papers that are not written or organized well, but they may not be able to tell students how to fix them. Most university professors are not trained for this, although they usually learn from experience how to recognize good writing when they see it. However, they may not be qualified to help you improve your writing skills.

One reason is because even though they have been teaching for many years and may have published books and articles, some professors don't write that well themselves. Many professors conduct research on specialized topics and write for limited audiences. Scholars in a particular discipline may have their own terms or jargon, and as long as they can string together sentences that use the accepted vocabulary, they can get by. If the professor doesn't have experience writing for a general audience, he or she may have a difficult time helping you with your writing.

At a minimum, professors should be able to recognize problems and direct you to the writing center on campus. But that is hardly an ideal solution. The writing center staff will be able to help with grammar and a few general rules of sentence construction and organization, but they probably can't help you write a better paper on American history unless they have studied that field.

The lack of basic writing skills is all the more troublesome because good writing only *begins* with correct use of the English language. It is not the goal. In fact, in an ideal world, every student would write competently from the first day of class so the professor can concentrate on the course material that will be the subject of the research papers and not how the papers are written and organized. Instead, professors have trouble seeing how much of the material students have learned because the writing often obscures their ideas.

> **It is not enough to gather information from various sources and put it in your paper. You have to show that you have your own ideas.**

You should attempt in every paper to clearly communicate your knowledge of the subject and demonstrate that you have thought creatively about the issues raised in your paper. Those are both difficult to do. But your professors want to see that you have acquired some knowledge through the research you have done and to see some of your ideas.

You cannot simply consult various sources and transfer the information you believe is relevant to the research paper. That doesn't require much thinking on your part. You need to show some analysis and interpretation of the information that reflects your thinking on the subject. Even if your ideas are not very sophisticated, the professor will likely appreciate that you did more than repeat what you read elsewhere.

Professors don't always read student papers carefully

The end of a semester is especially hectic for professors. They have to finish covering the course material, prepare exams and grade them, and read any papers that were due toward the end of the semester. If the class has more than 20 students, many professors will skim those papers. There just isn't time to read them thoroughly.

Professors may have only a few days between the time they have to give an exam and when they must turn in grades. The final exam schedule, which is established by the registrar's office, sets the time when exams will be given. Grades are almost always due Monday morning after finals week.

It is a nightmare for a professor with a class of 100 or 200 students when the final exam is scheduled for Thursday or Friday. That means the professor has only a few days to grade all the exams and any research papers that are still to be read, and to calculate all the grades for the class. In a class with a lot of students, there are not enough hours between the final exam and the submitting of the grades to do everything thoroughly.

Professors can't skimp on calculating the grades. They have to look at student grades throughout the semester, assign the proper percentage, and consider substantial improvement in borderline cases. Then all the grades must go on a data card or sheet that is sent to the registrar's office.

Where professors save time is by skimming the final papers or even the final exam if it is in an essay format. It probably doesn't surprise you to hear that professors don't always read every word carefully. If a professor makes at least some comments on the paper, you may never know how much of it was read.

If students write a 10-page research paper (many classes have longer papers), each paper will probably be 3,000 words. If there are 50 students in the class, the professor is supposed to read 150,000 words, the equivalent of two or three full-length books. It would take weeks to read them all thoroughly, plus the extra time to make comments on them.

Now that you know this, you can see how important it is to write clearly and to use good grammar. A professor reading that many papers a semester will be annoyed and distracted if he or she is slowed down by having to mark examples of bad grammar and incorrect spelling.

Students Sometimes Reject Advice on Their Writing

Professors make an interesting discovery after reading and commenting on student papers over a period of years. That discovery is that students who don't write well sometimes believe their writing is terrific and that a professor who criticizes that writing simply prefers a different style.

A professor may tell a student that a paper wasn't well organized, or that a particular paragraph was confusing, awkward, difficult to follow or didn't contribute to the overall essay. The student may react by believing that the paper was fine and the professor must be mistaken.

You may have been told throughout high school, and maybe in college as well, that there are a lot of ways to write, and you have probably been encouraged to develop your own "style." Your teachers and parents may have told you that your writing was good and improving when it was not. You may believe, therefore, that when your professor says your essay or research paper wasn't written well, what the professor doesn't recognize or appreciate is that you have a different way of writing it, and his or her way isn't better than yours, just different.

This can drive a professor crazy. Certainly there are different writing styles and there are many ways to convey information and express ideas. But when student writing is incoherent, awkward, and badly organized, with spelling and grammatical errors, the problem is not a difference in style. The problem is poor writing.

It may be natural to be defensive when a professor has handed back a paper with a lot of critical comments, or when the professor says in the office that there are serious problems with your writing. But don't assume that it is a difference in style. Look closely at your own writing and ask the professor to provide a sample of solid writing on the same subject so you can compare. Professors may have a copy of an essay exam or research paper from another semester that shows you the difference.

Television is the Scourge of Student Writing

Researchers have studied for years the impact of television on young people. By the time you are 18, you will have watched thousands of hours of TV. While watching TV, you are not reading books. In the old days, when students read more, they increased the chance that they would write better. They would have seen in books what good writing looks like, how sentences are written, how paragraphs are constructed, and how an overall theme is developed throughout the chapters.

Now, with students reading less, they are more likely to have writing problems. Since their foundation is weak, they have much further to go when it comes to improving their writing ability.

E-mail may also have had an impact on your writing. Because an e-mail message can be written and sent so quickly, it may be treated with less care than a letter. Once you get in the habit of dashing off quick e-mail notes without worrying about sentence structure or grammar, you may apply the same lack of care to your research papers and essay exams. Even professors send e-mails that don't reflect their best writing, and sometimes those habits find their way into the more formal work that they publish.

One way to deal with this is when you are reading for school or pleasure, pay attention occasionally to how the essay or book is written. See if you can get some hints on how to write better yourself by looking at how the author created sentences, structured paragraphs, and developed ideas.

Improvement Usually Comes Through Practice and Feedback

Despite the limited help that students sometimes get from their professors, their writing may improve over the time they are in college just because they continue to write more. Even with limited comments from professors, students often learn to research information better and to express themselves more clearly in papers and essays. Students would improve more quickly if they had active help, but generally student writing gets better during their undergraduate years.

If, however, you are having trouble with your writing and you are not getting enough feedback or personal attention, or you don't work hard at improving, your poor writing habits won't get corrected. I have taught seniors, for example, who misspell simple words on papers. I may ask them in my office if it was a typo or whether they really think the word is spelled that way. Too many times, the answer is the latter. I am curious how they could have gone all these years without knowing, for example, that "its" is used as a possessive pronoun, and "it's" is the contraction for "it is." I am surprised when they tell me that after high school and almost four years of college, no one has pointed this out before.

Employers Demand Writing Skills

Prospective employers frequently complain that those who graduate from universities lack basic writing skills. They also say that they don't have the time to teach those skills to new employees, even if they are otherwise bright and motivated. Some employers believe that students should take many more writing courses than they do.

The complaints are legitimate, but they don't always recognize certain realities about college. Students must be broadly educated and will therefore take a variety of courses from fields that don't require them to write. Depending on their major, some students may have limited opportunities to develop writing ability. For example, students rarely write papers in undergraduate math or science classes. Some students who dislike writing will avoid classes that include that as part of the course work.

This is frustrating for everyone. Almost any professional position requires writing skills. Whether it is writing memos to fellow employees or press releases for clients, or just a simple business letter, the ability to communicate clearly in writing is extremely important. Those who have those skills are often rewarded because employers recognize just how few people write well.

You should try to take as many classes as you can that will help you with your writing ability. If you learn to write well, it could make a difference in your career.

Keeping a Copy of Everything

Before you hand in a paper or take-home exam to a professor, you should make a copy of it. If you wrote it on your computer, it is probably enough to have a copy on a disk as long as you are not depending only on the original version on the hard drive.

A professor can misplace a paper at any time, but things are especially chaotic in the final days of the semester. To avoid a dispute over whether the paper was handed in, you must have a copy. You most likely will never need it, but when something goes wrong, you will be glad you have another copy to give the professor.

Handing in a Draft Even When It Is Not Required

Not enough students take advantage of this. Ask your professor if he or she will make comments on a draft of the paper so you can revise it. You have to make sure there is time for the professor to go over it, and get it back to you, before the due date. Many professors will agree to do this if you get it in early enough. You will almost always be able to improve the paper and get a better grade by revising it based on the teacher's comments, but it obviously requires you to do a draft earlier than you might otherwise.

Some teachers, however, discourage this practice. They believe it is unfair to the others in the class if you get the professor's comments on an early draft and then make changes to reflect those suggestions. Professors know that under ideal circumstances, every student would submit the paper early and get feedback on it. But if there are a lot of students in the class, the professor won't have time to do this.

Other teachers will respond positively to this show of initiative on your part and will make comments on a draft. After the paper has been assigned, contact the professor by e-mail, during office hours, or after the lecture, and ask if he or she will review a draft of the paper. Then write one as far in advance of the due date as you can.

This will be more productive if the draft is relatively polished and organized. At a minimum, the professor should be able to see most of the sources of information that you consulted and the main ideas you are discussing. If the first draft is in disarray, the professor will have to spend a lot more time going over it with you and may be left with a negative impression of your writing and commitment to doing a good paper. The more complete the draft, the more useful the feedback from the professor is likely to be.

Work on the Paper Soon After It Is Assigned

You will usually know the due date for a paper a month or more in advance. Yet instead of working on the paper steadily during the semester, some students will do almost all of it a few days before it is due.

Quite a few students seem to have a hard time working on something over a period of time. The papers they write would be more thoroughly researched, would be written better, and would have fewer mistakes if they worked on it over a period of weeks or longer.

Don't procrastinate. Work on your research papers steadily throughout the semester.

Sometimes there are good reasons for not working regularly on a paper for a particular class. You may have four other classes that semester where you are doing a lot of reading, preparing for exams, and writing papers. But when you know that a paper is not due for four more weeks, there seems to be little incentive to work on it steadily over that month. Professors can make judgments about the overall quality of the paper, but they have no way of knowing whether you worked on it for a few days or a few weeks.

You should try to be the exception to this rule. When you are assigned a paper, begin to do some of the research right away. This may be hard because the professor or textbook may not have covered the subjects that will be included in your paper and therefore, you may feel that you don't know enough to begin writing. But you should try to compensate for that by reading articles or portions of books that give you an overview of the subject.

Another reason for working on the paper early is you never know whether you will get extremely busy around the time the paper is due or get sick. Professors are sympathetic when you are sick for an exam. But they are likely to be more impatient when you have left to the last minute a paper that was assigned months ago and are feeling too ill to work on it a few days before it is to be turned in. In such a situation, you will be glad you worked on the paper in advance.

Getting Started

You need to follow several steps as you prepare to write a research paper. Not all of these will apply to every paper you write, but for most of the ones you will do for your classes, this is the process you should follow:

The first step is picking a topic. This is extremely important and more difficult to do than you may think. You should choose a topic that is appropriate for the length of the paper and the subject of the class. Here are some things to consider:

• How broad or narrow should the topic be?

If your research paper is going to be 10 pages, you cannot pick a broad topic and expect to cover it thoroughly. Such a paper would likely be superficial and will probably not show much original thinking about the subject because you won't have enough space.

You are probably better off choosing a narrow topic that you cover in more detail. If it is a topic more limited in scope, you may have the opportunity to offer some of your own ideas rather than just include information provided by others in books and articles and Internet materials.

The challenge is to find a topic that can be covered within the page limit, but not one that is so specialized that little information about it is available or no one would be interested in it.

You will need to do at least some research before you decide the scope of your project. This first step is necessary so you have some idea whether the topic is too broad or narrow. It is better to make this decision before you starting writing the paper.

- **Is there enough information available on the topic and where can it be found?**

Before choosing a subject for a research paper, you need to have some idea where materials are available. Use your computer to check the online catalog of your university's library. It is likely that there are books and journal articles and other materials in the library that would be helpful. If your library does not have some materials you need, they can be ordered through interlibrary loan. Because that may take a little time, you should begin working on your paper shortly after it is assigned.

Your university library may also make full-text databases available to students that provide excellent information on your topic. Go to your library's home page and look for a link to databases. If you don't see it, ask a librarian where on the Web site it is located.

Whether it is help with online resources or materials in the library, don't hesitate to ask a reference librarian for assistance. You may be surprised at how much information they can help you find on your subject.

- **Does the professor need to approve the topic before you begin the research?**

Some professors, especially if they are assigning longer papers, will ask students to submit a proposal or brief outline for the paper that has to be approved. But in many cases, professors don't require this.

Even if the professor doesn't say he or she must approve the topic in advance, you should write a brief description of the paper and see if the professor thinks it is a good idea. You should describe the topic, the sources available for information on that subject, and how you will approach the writing of the paper. A brief outline may be helpful.

Not enough students do this. If it turns out the topic wasn't appropriate, it may be too late to change after the student has spent a lot of time researching it. Then, when the professor reads the paper, he or she is likely to give it a lower grade because the topic doesn't fit well with the class or because it was too narrow or too broad. The professor will be able to help you find a topic that is right for the length of the paper and the subject of the class. That is likely to make your researching and writing easier and to result in a better paper.

• How do you do an outline?

It is amazing how many students seem to write research papers without doing an outline. You need to know in advance where your paper is going. You cannot write a coherent and well-organized research paper without an outline that indicates what topics and sub-topics will be covered and in what order.

Prepare a preliminary outline early in the research process. Create a list of topics that you think you will explore and place them in a logical order that reflects how you believe they should be discussed in the paper. Then research the topics beginning with the first one you plan to include. As your research continues, you will probably modify your outline. That is a normal part of the process. The important thing is that you have a plan and know where you are going with the paper. It is much better that way as compared with papers where you discuss whatever topic you happened to have read about last. If your paper is not organized well, you will probably not receive a good grade.

• Do you have to proofread the paper or just use the computer spell-checker?

You must proofread your paper very carefully and cannot assume that your computer program will catch all the spelling or grammar errors. A good research paper has no spelling errors and uses words correctly. Unfortunately, students don't always proofread their work carefully.

Many students assume, incorrectly, that as long as they have run the spell-check function on their computer, they don't need to proofread. As everyone knows who uses computers, the spell-checker only knows when a word is not in its dictionary. It doesn't know that you have used a real word, but it is not the one you wanted. Other mistakes you can make won't be detected by the spell-checker or grammar function on your computer.

**Proofread your papers carefully.
Incorrect spelling and poor grammar make
a bad impression and could affect your grade.**

Some students like to save the cost of printing drafts of their papers by trying to proofread while the text is on the computer screen. It is hard on your eyes to stare at a computer for long periods of time. Also with computers, you can only see a few paragraphs on the screen without scrolling and therefore, you may not get a good feel for how your paper flows and how the ideas are developed.

Spend the extra time and expense to print out your drafts and go over them carefully and mark changes with a pencil. You are likely to get a more complete picture of your paper and may find errors you wouldn't find on the screen.

Plagiarism

This is an extremely important topic, and students who are heading to college, or are already there, should be careful about how they gather and present information in essays or research papers. The consequences for breaking these rules and getting caught can be very serious. It is especially tempting to violate ethical standards because of how easy it is to copy text from the Internet.

In May 2001, a physics professor at the University of Virginia suspected that 122 of his students had copied sections of the research papers they wrote from online resources. The professor had created a computer program that scanned the students' papers for shared phrases of at least six words and compared them to the same phrases available on documents available through the Internet. Some students borrowed phrases or whole sections, and in a few cases, entire manuscripts, from online sources. (Lexington *Herald-Leader*, May 10, 2001, p. A 3 — Associated Press).

More than a thousand colleges and high schools subscribe to a service called "turnitin.com." When a teacher forwards an electronic version of the paper to the service over the Internet, it compares the paper with millions of Web sites and with papers that have been distributed by companies that write research papers for students for a fee. The founder of turnitin.com estimates that nearly one-third of the work submitted is copied in whole or in part from other sources. (Katie Hafner, "Lessons in the School of Cut and Paste," *New York Times*, June 28, 2001, p. D1.)

**If you are caught plagiarizing,
the consequences can be serious.**

The word plagiarism has a legal definition. According to Black's Law Dictionary, plagiarism is:

> The act of appropriating the literary composition of another, or parts or passages of his writings, or the ideas or language of the same, and passing them off as the product of one's own mind.

> To be liable for plagiarism it is not necessary to exactly duplicate another's literary work, it being sufficient if unfair use of such work is made by lifting of substantial portion thereof, but even an exact counterpart of another's work does not constitute plagiarism if such counterpart was arrived at independently.

It is easy to get caught

It is becoming easier than ever for professors to detect plagiarism. Professors may require students to provide a hard copy and an electronic version of the paper (either on disk or through e-mail). Plagiarism detection software then compares the phrases in the paper to Web sites and research papers in its database to see if students have copied phrases and sections of someone else's work.

Although cheating on exams also has serious consequences, it is often more difficult for a professor to discover. However, with plagiarism, the professor will frequently have solid evidence. He or she can place the student's paper next to the material allegedly copied from the Internet or some other source. If there is enough duplication, and especially if it doesn't sound like the student's work, the professor and university will have a strong case.

For almost every student, writing research papers is difficult. It takes time to gather the information and to write the paper in a way that is organized and fluent. When you are collecting information for the paper, you will encounter the writing of accomplished scholars and journalists whose work seems better than anything you could do at this stage. It is obviously tempting to use some of their phrases or entire paragraphs.

Since you may not know much about the topic you are researching, certainly compared with those who have studied the field for years, you may have trouble coming up with your own ideas about the subject. It is easy to "borrow" someone's ideas and later try to justify it by saying you discovered them on your own and are just saving time by using some of the author's words. Don't give in to this temptation. Always be careful about how you use and cite the works of others.

The Internet

Modern computer technology lets you do more extensive research more quickly than in any previous era. The amount of information available through the Internet is staggering. You have to know how to use search engines and to understand their limitations, but it is not hard to view text and sometimes pictures and graphics on almost any subject within minutes.

Remember that you can't always trust the information found on the Internet. Many people who create Web pages or offer other forms of Internet communication don't check the accuracy of the information. Certain sources you can trust without worrying much about their credibility but with other sites, you must treat the information with skepticism.

The Internet is a great source of information for your research papers, but it also makes it easy to copy someone else's work. With a few clicks of the keyboard and mouse, you can copy someone's words and paste them into your document or even download an entire paper written by someone else into your word processing program.

You may think you can justify such cut-and-paste copying by saying to yourself that you are simply gathering the information at this stage, and when you write the paper later, you'll make sure it is in your own words and reflects your own ideas. But it is tempting not to do that carefully later, especially if you are pressed for time or are having difficulty putting the thoughts into your own words.

Plagiarism is difficult to describe

Telling you how to avoid an accusation of plagiarism in the abstract is difficult. The line between safely using information you have gained from your research and illegitimately appropriating the work of others is not always clear.

It is the nature of writing papers that makes this so challenging. When you do a research paper for a college class, you will likely consult Internet and library resources to learn about the topic. With the Internet, you will probably download to your disk or printer words that have been written on the subject so you are not spending a lot of time taking notes.

Then you write a paper that reflects your ideas on the topic, and if you use specific information from another source, you are supposed to cite it in footnotes or endnotes or in the text. Many students who get caught plagiarizing and are facing punishment argue that what they did wrong was omit a citation and that such a "mistake" is minor. However, professors may see it as intentional cheating that deserves harsh punishment to teach that student a lesson and to deter others.

An example of plagiarism

Compare below the paragraph (in italics) that comes from the Web site of the National Archives and Records Administration about the Constitution and the Bill of Rights with the paragraphs that follow:

> *Madison's support of the bill of rights was of critical significance. One of the new representatives from Virginia to the First Federal Congress, as established by the new Constitution, he worked tirelessly to persuade the House to enact amendments. Defusing the anti-Federalists' objections to the Constitution, Madison was able to shepherd through 17 amendments in the early months of the Congress, a list that was later*

trimmed to 12 in the Senate. On October 2, 1789, President Washington sent to each of the states a copy of the 12 amendments adopted by the Congress in September. By December 15, 1791, three-fourths of the states had ratified the 10 amendments now so familiar to Americans as the "Bill of Rights."

(http://www.nara.gov/exhall/charters/constitution/conhist.html)

Now compare two ways that a student might use this information for a research paper on the Bill of Rights:

Sample #1

It was critical that Madison support a bill of rights. One of the new representatives to the first Congress from Virginia, he worked hard to persuade the House to enact amendments. Defusing the anti-Federalists complaints about the Constitution, Madison was able to steer 17 amendments through Congress in its early months, a number that was later trimmed to 12 in the Senate. President Washington sent to each of the states a copy of the 12 amendments on October 2, 1789. Three-fourths of the states had ratified 10 amendments, which Americans now know as the "Bill of Rights," by December 15, 1791.

Sample #2

It seems remarkable today that the delegates who wrote the Constitution would not have included a bill of rights, but they didn't. Maybe they believed the rights of the people were already protected in state constitutions, or that the new federal government had limited powers.

James Madison, a newly elected member of the U.S. House from Virginia, introduced the bill of rights in the First Congress and had to convince his colleagues that it should be passed. Eventually, the House approved 17

> amendments. The Senate must have rejected some amendments or combined them because it passed only 12 amendments. A little more than two years later, three-quarters of the states ratified the 10 amendments, known today at the "Bill of Rights."

Which sample do you think shows signs of plagiarism? The answer is #1.

In the first sample, the student used most of what was written on the NARA Web site and simply changed a few words ("complaints" instead of "objections") and moved a few phrases to different places in the sentences. Sample #1 looks like the student copied and pasted the paragraph and tried to disguise the plagiarism by making a few minor changes. It doesn't sound like student writing and there is nothing to indicate that the student had thought about the subject.

Even if sample #1 had a footnote indicating the source of the information to be the National Archives, the student still borrowed too heavily from the language of that Web site.

But in sample #2, the student begins by commenting on the fact that the delegates to the Constitutional Convention didn't include a bill of rights when they wrote the Constitution. The student may not know why they failed to do this but is willing to speculate about that. This was not explicitly stated in the paragraph from the Web site, but the student figured out that because Congress was approving a bill of rights, it had not been done at the Convention. Professors want students to make these discoveries on their own.

The student also doesn't know why the Senate reduced the number of proposed amendments from 17 to 12 (in reality, no one does because the Senate met behind closed doors at the time and the debate is not reflected in the Senate journal) but is guessing that the Senate thought there were too many and that some had to be eliminated or combined. Once again, the student seems to be thinking about the information and is not just transferring sentences that someone else wrote.

Also, the second paragraph of sample #2 is written more in the student's words, although the student uses the facts provided in the Web site. If the student referred to the NARA Web site as the source of the facts in a footnote or endnote or in the text, sample #2 would clearly be acceptable in a paper and is the student's work.

When it comes to doing citations, you should check with the professor to see what form he or she prefers. Ask for a sample of citations for books, articles, and the Internet so you can do them correctly.

You can cite sources and still be guilty of plagiarism

Some students believe that as long as they identify the source of the information, they can use anything that someone has written. The problem is that quotation marks, footnotes or endnotes don't always make clear what is the students' work and what is the work of someone else.

Much of the time, you will summarize what a writer has said and integrate that information into your research paper. But if you inappropriately use material that someone else has written, you are not likely to make it clear in the footnote or endnote where the ideas or words of the source you are citing ended and where your words or ideas began. Just attaching a footnote number next to someone else's words does not mean you are free from a charge of plagiarism.

Here's an example: You take someone's exact words and place them in your paper. You put a footnote number at the end of the paragraph, but you don't use quotation marks to indicate those words were written by someone else.

What does the reader think when seeing that footnote number? Most likely, the reader believes that those words are *yours,* while the idea you are discussing was inspired by the work of someone else whose name you are citing in the foot-note text. If, on the other hand, you stole the writer's exact words and simply cited the source of the information, there is no way for the reader to know the words were not yours. That would be plagiarism even though there was a citation identi-fying the source of the information.

In early 2002, news reports revealed that experienced and respected historians had used sections of previous books without proper attribution. These historians used the words of other authors, and although they may have cited that au-thor in a footnote, the historians failed to use quotation marks to show the words were written by someone else.

As a result of the revelations, some books had to be re-called and some of the historians were sharply criticized in the press. This shows you that even accomplished writers make this mistake and that the consequences can be serious.

Ask for help

In my 20 years of teaching, I cannot remember a time when a student came to see me before a paper was due to ask me about how to avoid a plagiarism problem. For example, no one has brought a newspaper or journal article, book, or printout from the Internet from which they gathered infor-mation and asked me how to discuss and cite it without pla-giarizing the source.

Now that Internet resources have been available for a num-ber of years, you should ask your teachers to talk more about how to avoid plagiarism issues before they assign a paper. See if they will provide examples so you and your classmates will be able to recognize the line between good research and writing and improperly using someone else's work.

The fear of false accusation

Students may worry about being falsely accused of plagia-rism and having a difficult time defending themselves. How do you prove that words or ideas were your own? Obviously, if you lifted whole sections or an entire paper from someone else and the professor found that document on the Internet or in a book or article, you don't have much of a defense. There will also be cases where no specific source could be found, but where the professor strongly suspects that it is not the student's work.

A professor has to be cautious about accusing a student of plagiarism. A false accusation that embarrasses a student may lead to a lawsuit or disciplinary action against the teacher. Professors and the university administrators who deal with these issues must have solid, almost irrefutable, evidence of plagiarism before taking action against a student.

This doesn't mean that you don't have to worry about being caught when you have done something wrong. It means that as long as you have used the information in your paper in an appropriate manner, the chances of being accused and punished are small. Only in the most clear-cut cases with strong evidence will administrators take action against a student.

To help support your defense in a plagiarism case, you may want to show the notes you took while doing the research. Keep those notes in a file until at least the end of the semester.

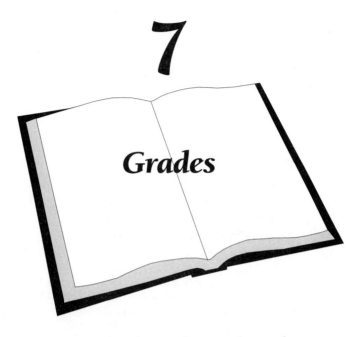

7

Grades

Summary: This chapter discusses how to keep grades in perspective and how to avoid worrying too much about them.

Why It Matters: Grades are important, but getting good grades does not mean you are getting a good education.

Some students concentrate so much on getting high grades that they forget that grades are supposed to *reflect* what you learn and are not the goal of a college education. It is not necessarily your fault if you over-emphasize the importance of grades. Your parents may believe that it is the sole measure of success in college, and they may put a lot of pressure on you to maintain a high GPA. You may want good grades to get into graduate or professional school or to keep a scholarship.

As professors would readily admit and as experienced college students already know, the assigning of grades is, to say the least, an inexact science. Most of the time, the grade you receive at the end of the semester will be derived directly from the grades you were given on exams and papers and for class participation. But a number of factors can affect how the individual assignments are graded, and they will obviously impact on the final grade. Some factors that have little to do with your scores during the semester could also affect your grade.

Grades create a lot of anxiety for students. You may feel that the grade you received on an exam or paper didn't reflect the amount of time you spent preparing for the test or researching and writing the paper. That often bothers students, but the professor may have no way of knowing how hard you worked. Or you may feel that your exam and paper were very good, but that the professor failed to appreciate or recognize the quality of your work.

The purpose of going to college is to learn and no matter what grades you receive, it is what you get out of your courses and outside activities that matter.

For students who apply to graduate or professional school, their GPA will be an important factor in determining whether they are admitted. In addition, some employers screen resumes based on GPA. But even the pursuit of high grades has to be balanced with the primary purpose of being in college.

Grades Don't Matter That Much

Coming from a professor, the above statement may be unexpected. But there is entirely too much concern about grades. If you think only about the grade you will get for the course and how it will affect your overall average, you may learn less from a class than you would otherwise if you concentrated more on what you are studying. There are several reasons why you should worry less about grades and more about what you are learning in a class.

Employers and grades

You and your parents may be surprised to learn that relatively few employers look at a transcript or consider your grades when making a hiring decision. It is true, of course, that the human resources staff at some large companies that receive a lot of resumes will sometimes screen applicants by GPA. Those with higher grades have a greater chance of being interviewed although not necessarily a better chance of being hired.

If particular subjects matter to an employer, it is possible you will be asked to show what grades you earned in certain classes. A public school district, for example, before hiring a teacher for a biology position may want to know what grades that applicant received in biology and other science courses. But the district knows that just because a student received a "B" in a college course doesn't mean he or she is less qualified to teach that subject than a student who received an "A". There are too many factors that affect grades.

Employers usually look at a lot more than grades when hiring someone. For example, which of the two students below is more likely to be hired to work on the staff of a member of Congress?

> *Student #1*
> Almost all "A's" in political science classes.
> No outside activities.

> *Student #2*
> Almost all "B's" in political science classes.
> Interned in Washington, D.C. on Capitol Hill.
> Belongs to a campus political organization.
> Has worked in a political campaign and registered voters.

Almost certainly Student #2 would be hired before Student #1.

Most employers are interested in the skills, knowledge and experience you acquired while in college and seeing that you are mature and responsible. It is your overall experience and how you have benefited from that experience that matter the most. If you concentrate almost exclusively on grades, you may miss the opportunity to do the other things that are more important than your grades.

As you plan your college studies and your career, talk to professors, alumni, or prospective employers at job fairs about how much grades matter when you apply for a job. It may help you to find the right balance between grades and other activities.

Grades have no impact on what you learn in a class

Students who receive a "C" in one of my classes have sometimes told me how hard they studied for the course. They explain how many hours they spent reading the textbook, that they did not miss any of the lectures, that they spent a lot of time preparing for the exams, and worked diligently on the research paper. Then they will sometimes add that they got a lot out of the course and they want me to know that the grade they received did not accurately reflect how much they learned.

It is gratifying to hear such a comment, and it underscores an important point about college classes: When a professor enters a grade on the grade sheet at the end of the semester, that act has no effect whatsoever on what a student learned in the class. When students come to see me after being disappointed with their grade, I point out that no one can take away what they got out of the class. Whether I write a "C" or an "A" on the grade form does not change that at all.

Obviously, you may feel better about a course or it may help your self-confidence if you receive an "A" instead of a "C." And self-confidence matters both while you are in college and when you graduate and pursue a career. But long after you have left the university, what is important is that you learned the material, developed some of your own ideas about the subject, improved your writing skills, and were inspired to learn more, not what grade you received.

Not every student and parent understands this. Students sometimes believe that if they get a lower grade than they expected or thought they deserved, it means they got less out of the class. If you think about this rationally, however, you will realize that anything a professor does after the class has ended will have no impact on what you learned.

Grades don't always show what you learned in the class

Not only does the assigning of the grade not *affect* what you learned in the class, it may not accurately *reflect* what you learned. This is something that many students and parents don't realize. You can learn a lot in classes where you received a mediocre grade and learn little from a course in which you got an "A."

Grades are usually a calculation of your scores on the exams, quizzes, papers, other written assignments, and sometimes factors such as class attendance and class participation. When the professor looks at your grades over the semester, he or she will apply the percentage allocated to each assignment as established in the syllabus and come up with a final grade. In those instances when you are on the border between one grade and another, the teacher may consider whether you improved the quality of your work over the semester, whether you seemed to be trying hard, or whether you came to the professor's office during the semester to discuss the class. Sometimes your demeanor or attitude toward the class or whether the professor likes you as a person may be a factor, although teachers try not to let those matters affect the grade they assign.

If a grade is to accurately reflect what you got out of the class, each exam would have to test your knowledge of the subject in a way that directly demonstrated what you learned. For reasons that were described in a previous chapter, exams can test only a small part of the material that is covered during the semester, and even students who study conscientiously don't do well on certain exams.

To illustrate this point, think about a student who studies the topics 1, 2, 3, 4, and 5 for the first exam. But the exam tests 4, 5, 6 and 7. The student understands topics 1–5, but did not get the opportunity on the exam to show he or she knows all that material. Thus, the grade would be lower than if the student had studied exactly the right issues. Regardless of whether the subjects were included on the test, the student still learned about them.

Or, perhaps you studied all the right subjects, yet the questions on the exam did not ask for the kind of responses you prepared. You still know the material even though the exam did not include the precise questions that would show how much you had studied and learned.

What this means is that grades on exams don't always show how much you are learning and thus the final grade, which is based on exam scores, may not demonstrate what you got out of the course.

It is important not to overdo this point. If I give three exams during the semester, and one student gets a 70 on each, while another student gets a 90 on every test, it is probably safe to assume that the student with the 90 is learning more from the course than the student with the lower grade. But you and your parents should not assume that a lower score on one exam shows either a lack of commitment on your part or that you are not learning the material.

The Pursuit of Grades Can Negatively Affect What You Learn

Students who approach every class with the idea that they will do whatever they need to get high grades may not get as much as they could from the course. Two potential problems exist: One, students will study only the material that they think will be on the exam. And two, what material they do study will be approached only in the context of how to prepare for tests and not for the long term.

Studying only material that will be on the tests

If you approach every course with the idea that you will study only what you believe will be on the exams, with the sole purpose to get a good grade, you will have missed much of what college offers. We have gone over this point before in earlier chapters but a few things are worth mentioning again.

You have a limited amount of time to devote to each class. If you are taking five courses during the semester, working part-time, are involved in extra-curricular activities and are trying to have a social life, you have to budget your time carefully.

Recognizing that there are only a fixed number of hours you can devote to each course, if you are studying only what you need to know for the exam, then you are not necessarily studying what you need to know for your career or life.

These two issues are obviously not mutually exclusive. In other words, if you read the textbooks and listen to the lectures with an eye toward what you will need to know for the first test, you are probably learning much of what the course is potentially offering you over the long term. However, many subjects that are discussed in the textbook and lectures, or considered in the supplemental readings, are not going to be on the exam.

My class in media law exposes students to a lot of court cases and issues. Only a small number of those will be tested. However, I constantly say to students that if a case mentioned in the lecture or textbook sounds interesting to them, they should take a little time to look at it even if it won't be tested. They can't read all of these cases, of course, but they should read at least some.

Unfortunately, once the students know that the additional case that was discussed in class or mentioned in the book will not be on the exam, it is extremely unlikely that someone in the class will take the time to read it. I know this to be true because when students do occasionally look at material that won't be on the exam, they usually tell me without being asked. Also, I will ask the class after mentioning an important case to see if anyone looked at it. Several semesters pass before a single hand is raised with a positive response to that question.

Some of this may be laziness. The students may have the time to explore some additional subjects that won't be on the test. They just don't want to make the effort. But for many students who have hectic schedules and little time to devote to each class, it is all they can do to study the material for the exam. They feel any additional reading is a luxury they can't afford.

That is not the way to approach college. You obviously cannot ignore the material that will be on the tests and instead explore peripheral or secondary issues the whole semester. But you need to think of college as a learning adventure. You have 15 weeks with the professor and the other students in the class. You need to ask "What can I do during this semester to get everything out of this class that I can?" The answer is not to do the minimum work required, to study only what will be on the exams, and not to seek out information on non-exam topics.

Focusing only on the exams also
affects how you learn the material

Many exams require you to memorize certain facts or principles that are discussed in the textbook or lectures. But just memorizing words and repeating them on the exam doesn't mean that you have learned anything or that you have done any thinking about the issues that underlie those facts.

For example, my students read a 1973 Supreme Court decision in which the Court tried to define obscenity. Legislatures and courts must provide as clear a definition as possible so those who create, distribute or use sexually explicit materials will know in advance what is permissible and what is illegal.

The students know that I will ask them on the in-class exam to cite the Court's definition of obscenity from that case. Not surprisingly, the students do a great job memorizing each of the definition's three parts. Many of them can repeat the Supreme Court's exact words. However, just because the students are able to memorize words from a Supreme Court decision does not mean they understand the complex issues related to the Court's obscenity rulings.

No professor should be satisfied with students merely memorizing words. Those of us who teach media law want to know that our students have formed some judgment of their own about how society and courts should decide what is obscene. But if students know they will only have to repeat the words of the Court's definition on the exam, that is usually what they will study for the test and not go any deeper.

> **You remember more when**
> **you think and don't just memorize.**

Here is why it makes a difference. Students will likely forget the exact words of the obscenity definition within days, or hours, after the exam has ended. If, instead, they had thought about what the words actually mean and how they should be applied to future circumstances, they would more likely remember that experience much longer than they will the words of the definition.

It is this learning *experience*—the discovery on your own of concepts and facts, and the ability to synthesize and analyze and think critically about the issues raised by those facts—that will make a difference in your career and your life. If someday you need the exact words of the Supreme Court's definition of obscenity, you will easily be able to look them up. The much harder task of thinking creatively and critically and coming up with your own ideas is what is really more important and will stay with you past graduation day.

If you are only "learning" what you think will be on the exam, you will have no incentive to go beyond memorizing facts. You will never attempt the more challenging task of developing your analytical skills and figuring out how to apply those facts to various situations. If the test asks for you to memorize words and you do that well, you may get an "A" in the class. You and your parents should not assume, however, that the high grade you received means you learned very much.

Stress from worrying about grades

The emphasis on grades can affect how you learn in a physical way. Students are often under a lot of stress. People mistakenly believe that undergraduates lead a near-blissful existence. They don't have to be concerned about "grown-up" issues such as a difficult job, the mortgage, kids who get sick, car payments and income taxes that take too much of their paycheck, health insurance costs, and a hundred other things.

Some people outside of universities think that all students do is go from one class to another, visit friends, attend parties and athletic events, stay up late, sleep late, study when they feel like it, and generally have a good time for four years.

This description would apply to a small minority of students. Many undergraduates are under incredible pressure. They are taking four or five classes, some of which may be very hard. Their professors may not do a good job presenting the material or even explaining the requirements.

Far from a happy and carefree social life, students are sometimes lonely and have a difficult time meeting people with whom they can be friends. Boyfriend and girlfriend problems can be serious and upsetting.

Undergraduates, like everyone else, worry about money. They may have physical and emotional problems. They may have a tense and uncomfortable relationship with their parents. They may dislike a part-time job for which they are paid little and may worry about many other things.

Students today also think a lot about careers. They know that in many fields they will be competing for jobs with other bright and motivated students from their own schools and from colleges around the country. They worry about what they will do when they graduate.

If you add the anxiety over grades to all this, you can see that many students are under a strain. A few chapters ago, I mentioned the conversation with the parents of an incoming freshman who demanded that their daughter maintain at least a 3.0 GPA every semester or they would refuse to pay for her schooling. Do you think that student will approach her courses with the idea of exploring how they can enrich her life or will she be thinking about what is required to get good grades so her parents won't cut her off?

Sadly, some parents have convinced their children that if they get lower than expected grades, the parents will be disappointed in them. When you are 18, on your own and away at college for the first time, you may have a lot of concerns about your ability to succeed in college and beyond. Some experiences in college in the early months will help you build self-confidence and will motivate you. Other experiences will make you wonder whether you have the ability to make it.

Parents should not add to this apprehension by establishing firm rules for grades. The first semester or two can be incredibly difficult. Students get homesick, they miss a boyfriend or girlfriend who was left behind or moved elsewhere, they don't like their living situation, and they may not have made any friends. And to top it off, they are taking calculus!

They should keep their parents informed on how they are doing in school and should share grade reports with them at the end of each semester. But parents must consider why their children may be off to a difficult start when it comes to grades. No arbitrary grade point cutoff should be established. Students have enough pressure on them. Parents should not add to that by making their children feel they will be a disappointment if they don't get all high grades.

This doesn't mean, however, that if they get a "D" or an "F" that it is okay because they still got something out of the class. What I am saying is that students and parents need to concentrate on what is being learned, not grades.

Every Student Should Get a Few Lower Grades

This sounds like a strange thing to say, but I think it would be healthy for almost every student to get at least a few "C's". If a student has a very high GPA, he or she may feel intense pressure to get all A's. Getting a lower grade once in a while may take some of the strain off because the GPA would no longer be pristine and have to be so carefully protected.

Too many students decide which classes to take and how to study the material in the class based solely on grades. Even worse, some students drop a class when they think they may get a "C" even if half of the semester is over. In such a situation, the student often takes it again, sometimes from the same teacher, or substitutes another class that will satisfy the requirement.

Ironically, the students who worry the most about grades are often the ones with the highest GPA. I occasionally encounter students who have made it to their junior or senior year with a perfect 4.0. They believe that everything they do, from deciding which classes to take, to how to study for exams, must be directed toward keeping that 4.0.

Because of the way they approach their classes, students who consistently get very high grades may be "enjoying" college less than almost anyone at the university. Every course, every teacher, every subject within the course, and every exam and paper, is looked at through the sole focus of how to get an "A." They won't allow themselves the luxury of exploring issues that won't be on the exam. They may believe they don't have time to work on the school newspaper or get involved in one of the other worthwhile activities at a university.

If they ever receive a "B" or a "C", and don't have a coronary, it may actually do them some good. Think of the professional baseball pitcher who has a no-hitter going into the seventh inning. Unless that player is more like a machine than a person, he will feel tremendous stress until someone gets a single. Although he will be disappointed, he will be able to relax some and enjoy himself more. The stress of maintaining a no-hitter is over.

Students who had a 4.0 may enjoy school more after they have gotten their first "B." In the end, of course, it won't matter much anyway. Out of 120 credits, one or two "B's" won't make much difference, perhaps less than one-tenth of one point (they may end up with a 3.95 instead of 4.0).

Professors who serve on the admissions committees for graduate schools and professional schools and prospective employers should be a little suspicious of students with a 4.0.

They are obviously bright and hard-working, but have they done anything else in college that would make them well-rounded and interesting? This is not a criticism of students who study hard and receive good grades. But getting high grades is not the reason to go to college. The purpose is to learn, to be inspired, to mature, and to enjoy new and exciting experiences.

Challenging Grades

There may be a time when you feel you received a lower grade than you deserved. If you think a grade was unfair, go see the professor. However, you should not try to negotiate grades with your teacher. You need to make your case based on how the exam questions reflected the material in the class or where in your research paper you did what the professor had said students needed to do. But do not tell your professor that you need a higher grade to get into graduate school or because your parents will be angry if your GPA falls below a certain level.

If the professor thinks a mistake has been made, he or she will change your grade. Even if that doesn't happen, you will get an explanation that will tell you what you did wrong and how to better prepare for the next exam or paper.

Some students mistakenly believe that the head of the department serves as an "appellate judge" for grades. There is, however, a basic tenet in the academic world that the person who is teaching the class should assign the grades. It is highly unusual, and very controversial, for the department chair to change a grade over the objections of the professor who teaches the class.

Grade Inflation

At many universities, more students are receiving very high grades than used to in the past. Unless today's students are much brighter and more motivated than those of, let's say, 20 years ago, the difference is explained by professors giving "A's" for work that would have earned a "B" some time ago, or a "B" today for the equivalent of "C" work in the past. This is known as grade inflation.

The value of high grades decreases if so many students are receiving them. If you are in a class of 100 students, your "A" means a lot if only five students in the class received one. But if 50 students got an "A," your grade doesn't seem so special anymore.

At Harvard University, among the best and most prestigious colleges in the country, almost half the grades awarded in recent years, 49 percent, were either "A" or "A–." Failing grades, D's and C's accounted for fewer than 6 percent. ("A's Soar at Harvard, Nearing a Majority," *New York Times*, Nov. 22, 2001, p. A22; "Woe Is Harvard, Where All Are Above Average," *New York Times*, Dec. 5, 2001, p. A14). In 1986, 23 percent of the grades were an "A" or "A–." (Richard Rothstein, "Doubling of A's at Harvard: Grade Inflation or Brains?" *New York Times*, Dec. 5, 2001, p. A21).

Just as startling is this figure: 91 percent of Harvard students graduated with honors in June 2001. ("Why Grade Inflation Is Serious," *New York Times* editorial, Dec. 9, 2001, p12). Grade inflation is a problem not just at Harvard, but at many universities.

Educators have argued for years about how serious a situation grade inflation is, what causes it, and what can be done about it. Some professors have tried to maintain traditional grading standards by giving a majority of students a "C" in the class, and saving the "B's" and "A's" for exemplary work.

That is a problem if some professors adhere to such standards while others don't. If students know that Professor Jones gives many "C's" while Professor Smith, who teaches a different section of the class, follows more "modern" grading standards, the students will do everything they can to avoid Professor Jones's class. If Professor Jones has consistently low enrollment compared with the classes of colleagues, university administrators may think there is something wrong with his or her teaching. That perception could affect the professor's chances of gaining tenure and promotion and may affect pay increases.

A professor can't fight grade inflation alone

All professors within a department or college, or throughout the entire university, would have to impose relatively uniform standards if they want to resist grade inflation. The problem is that uniform standards don't exist. What is "B" work for one professor in one course would be considered "C" work in another professor's class. Professors are not machines, and even the same course is not taught the same way by every professor. We could impose uniform standards by having all students learn the material by computer and take the same test, but that hardly seems like a reasonable response to this problem.

The pressure on professors to give good grades

Professors generally recognize that if they give very many "C's," they will spend more time dealing with student complaints than they would if they gave higher grades. More students will make appointments to see them in the office to dispute the grade, and they will spend more time explaining why a student did not get all the points they expected on a particular answer and discussing how the final grade was calculated.

There is a dispute among professors over whether lower grades affect how students evaluate the quality of the teaching and the course. At the end of the semester, but before final exams, students fill out an evaluation form about their teacher.

Most universities take teaching evaluations very seriously. A professor who gets mediocre scores on the evaluation may be denied tenure or promotion, may get smaller pay increases or none at all, may be perceived as ineffective, and may be denied the chance to teach popular courses. Most professors would admit that if they are a tough grader and students see that their exam and paper scores may be leading to a "C," some students will show their displeasure by giving low scores and making negative comments on the teaching evaluation.

This is obviously not true all the time, and some professors who say they are extremely demanding and actually give "C's" or "D's" are nevertheless very popular. But many professors would argue that they see a relationship between the grades they give and the teaching evaluation scores.

Since almost every student gets mostly "A's" and "B's," you and your parents may not be able to determine how much you are getting out of each course based on the grade. You have to approach each course with the idea of learning as much as you can and not by focusing exclusively on the grade.

The Grading System Is Part of the Problem

During the course of my academic career, I have taught at universities that use different grading systems. At one of the universities, we could give a grade down to the one-tenth point. Thus a student's final grade could be 2.6, 2.7, 3.1, 3.2, or 3.9. That was probably too precise. When a professor calculated the grades, a very small difference on one of the exams, perhaps no more than one point out of a hundred, could make the difference between 3.5 or 3.6.

At other universities, we have been able to give letter grades with pluses or minuses. In those institutions, a student could be given a final grade of a "B+" or an "A–." That provided some important flexibility that I miss, because at my current university, we can only give whole letter grades.

Under such a system, a student who receives a 79 and one who gets an 89 are both likely to get a "B" in the class. A professor may give the student with an 89 a "B" to reserve the "A's" for those few students who really did terrific work. The student with the 79 will probably get a "B" because he or she will otherwise demand to know why the dreaded "C" instead of a "B" was assigned when it was that close. A teacher may not want to spend the time explaining it to the disgruntled student and will just give the "B" to head off the meeting to discuss the grade.

Students should ask their professors early in the semester how they determine grades and whether there are factors that are not explained in the syllabus that may make a difference. For example, the syllabus may not say that class attendance or class participation may affect the grade. When students are at a college that does not allow pluses or minuses, they should talk to their professors about grading. A very small difference in performance over the semester may determine the final grade in borderline cases.

Personal Factors

Professors are human. Although almost all professors try to be fair, there are always going to be some students whom teachers get to know and like as people and some they like less.

When professors consider personal factors, which they probably shouldn't, they almost always do so in the direction of helping the student. In other words, when a student is on the border between a "C" and "B," professors are more likely to give the student a "B" if they have gotten to know the student and have seen how hard he or she worked in the class, than they are to give the student a "C" because there was a

Research Databases A-Z

A to Z: The World -geography, cultures
ABI/INFORM Complete -business
Academic Search Premier (EBSCO) Full-text, scholarly peer-reviewed periodicals, "Number of Pages" widget
Access Science (McGraw Hill) -encycl.
ARTstor -paintings, sculptures, etc.
Asian American Drama (Alexander)
Black Drama (Alexander)
Blackwell Encycl. Sociology (Wiley)
Britannica Image Quest -rights-cleared
Business Source Elite (EBSCO)
Chronicle of Higher Education
CINAHL (EBSCO) nursing journals
Comm. & Mass Media (EBSCO) -journals
CQ Researcher -experts / pro/con
Credo Reference 650+ encycl. Ref.
Criminal Justice (ProQuest) 240 journals
Dentistry and Oral Sciences Source
Diagnostic Stat. Man. Mental Disorders (DSM-5) (APA) -definitive handbook
EBSCOhost eBooks 1000s of e-books,
EBSCO Complete -search 20+ databases
Encyclopedia Britannica 73,000 articles
Epocrates -disease basics, diagnosis, etc.
ERIC (EBSCO) -education journals
Films on Demand 14,000+ videos
Fire Technology Leading journal, fire safety
Gale Virtual Reference Library -100s encyclopedias, dictionaries, ref.
Health Source: Consumer (EBSCO) -popular

Health Source: Nursing (EBSCO) -clinical
Historical Newspaper Collection 5 majors
Hoover's Company Profiles –priv. & public firms
Hospitality and Tourism (EBSCO) –journals
HRAF Archaeology / HRAF World Cultures Yale
Intl. Encycl. of Dance (Oxford) ~2000 articles
Issues and Controversies on File (Facts on File) -pro & con, controversial topics
JADA: Journal of the Am. Dental Assoc.
JAMA: Journal Am. Medical Association
Journal Am. Animal Hospital Association
JSTOR -archive scholarly journals > 1800s
Kanopy Videos 100s doc./educational films
Las Vegas/Nev. News (Newsbank) newspapers
Learning Express - Practice Tests -nursing, Praxis, GED, ASVAB, ACT, SAT, etc.
LexisNexis Academic includes Shepard's Citations
Literature Criticism Online (Gale) -scholarly
Literature Resource Center (Gale) -overviews, reviews, criticism, bios, multi-media, etc.
MasterFILEPremier -mags, Consumer Reports
MEDLINE (EBSCO) National Library of Medicine
National Geographic Archive 1888-present
Nature –renowned, peer-reviewed, science/tech
Newspaper Source Plus –many national/interntl
Newsstand -over 1,300 newspapers
North American Theatre Online -plays, people, +
North American Women's Drama (Alexander)
Nursing & Allied Health Source (ProQuest) -radiography, PT, dietetics, dental hygiene

Opposing Viewpoints in Context (Gale) Pro & con articles: contemporary social issues
Ovid Nursing Journals 50 journals
Oxford Encycl. Food and Drink in America
Oxford English Dictionary (Oxford)
Physicians' Desk Reference –best drug info
Professional Development Coll. (EBSCO)
Pronunciator -learn 80 languages
ProQuest Central -journals, mags, etc.
PsychARTICLES (APA) -full txt, peer-reviewed
Psychology & Behavioral Sciences Collection (EBSCO) 530+ peer-reviewed journals
PubMed Central -biomedical research
Regional Business News -newspapers, wires
Religion & Philosophy Collection (EBSCO)
Safari Tech Books Online 20,000 ebooks: computers, technology, software, digital media
Science (journal) –renowned scientific resrch
Scientific American (magazine) –renowned full text, scholarly, but not peer-reviewed
SciFinder renowned source on chemistry
Sources in U.S. History: Slavery (Gale)
Sources in U.S. History: Civil War (Gale)
SpringerLink e-books & journals, sci. & med.
State Stats -current & historical data 50 states
Twayne's Author Series -literary authors/works
Twentieth Century North American Drama
U.S. History in Context -primary sources
UNLV Digital Collections -local history archive
Vocational & Career (EBSCO) -trade & industry

Your CSN Libraries

www.csn.edu/library

Discover
Connect
Inspire

Research Help–Personalized: visit your campus libraries (CH, NLV, HN), call 702-651-4419, chat online, or email for help finding articles/books/films/more.

Research Help–Online
*Citation tools: MLA, APA, KnightCite
*Sample MLA, APA essays/term papers
*Easy online research tutorials

Off-campus Access: to read articles and ebooks off-campus, use your NSHE student ID # for the username and your Canvas password (this CAN be different from My CSN password). Instructors and staff use CSN email credentials. Login problems? Call CSN Help Desk 702-651-4357

Free CSN Library Card
*Show photo id & tell your NSHE student ID #
*Textbooks at Circ. Desk: 2-hour use
*3500+ kids' books for 3-week checkout

NLV Campus Library Hours:
Mon-Thu: 7:30 –9:00 PM
Fri: 7:30-4:00 PM closed Sat, Sun

personal dislike. Some professors believe it is all right to give a break to a student who has shown a genuine interest in the class.

Students rarely have any control over this. If they don't like the course, or think it is boring, or don't like the teacher, they should avoid expressing that sentiment to the professor too harshly. On the other hand, they should not go to a professor's office if the only purpose is to tell the professor how wonderful he or she is and how stimulating the course is in the hope that this will influence grades.

Professors want students to come to class every day, to be excited about the material, to keep up with the reading, to ask good questions, and (professors never stop hoping) to be interested in issues in the class even when they are not going to be on the exam.

Part III

8

Your Relationship with Professors

Summary: This chapter discusses how to interact with professors to get the most out of your relationship with them.

Why It Matters: Professors not only teach you the substantive material, they can help you in a variety of ways while you are in school and after you graduate.

When you are in college, you will get advice on everything from what classes to take to how to plan for your career. What you are not likely to hear much about is how to develop a positive relationship with your professors that will help make your college experience more satisfying.

Universities don't provide information about this in the bulletin or advising materials, and few professors discuss with their students what kind of relationship they should have for several reasons.

One is that some professors and administrators may not think it is very important. They may have the attitude that you are expected to attend class, take notes, study for exams, write papers, graduate, get a job, and then contribute money to the university. There doesn't seem to be an obvious need to discuss how you should interact with professors.

Another reason is that professors have a variety of teaching styles and they deal with students in different ways, so general advice would not necessarily apply to a specific situation. Some faculty members are formal, and students can tell just by the professor's demeanor that this is not someone whose office you will pop in without an appointment to have a casual chat. Other professors are informal in their appearance, personality, and attitude, and you will have the chance to get to know them and to talk to them candidly.

Although students get little guidance on how to deal with their professors, it is nevertheless a very important relationship. Professors are in a position to help you in many different ways. While you are still an undergraduate, they can recommend you for a scholarship that could help pay for some of your last year or two of school. They can enrich your learning experience by inviting you to special events that few students are allowed to attend. There you may meet interesting people from inside and outside the university who may become valuable contacts later.

Students whom professors like and think have great promise may benefit just by being able to spend more time talking with their teachers in their office about the classes they are taking and their career aspirations.

Professors can write you a letter of recommendation for graduate school or a professional program, and even pick up the phone to call an old friend or colleague if they are especially enthusiastic about your prospects. Such an endorsement could make the difference in whether you are accepted to a competitive program.

Professors can recommend students they admire to prospective employers and provide contact information that they wouldn't give to someone who is less motivated.

Obviously, professors can't do these things, or at least not enthusiastically, unless they have gotten to know you. You should make an effort to get to know at least some professors while you are an undergraduate. Do not just attend class. You may be missing out on some important benefits of being in college.

The Foundation of a Good Relationship

Some professors talk about these matters to their classes or to individual students, but many times students don't know how to develop an appropriate relationship with a professor. Here are a few things to keep in mind:

How to address your professors

Professors should tell their students the first day of class how they want to be addressed. If they don't, students may have to ask or guess, and that may be awkward.

If your professor doesn't say anything about what he or she wants to be called, you need to abide by the long standing tradition of not calling someone by his or her first name unless you are told to do so. It is something your parents probably discussed with you when you were growing up. Most likely, you never called your teachers by their first name when you were in high school.

But for some reason, perhaps because of the informal era in which we live, some students believe it is acceptable to address professors the same way they do their friends. Once in a while, either in class or in an e-mail or a written note, one or more of my students makes this mistake. When I call on students in class to see what questions they have, I don't expect to hear "Richard, would you go over that material again? I didn't understand it."

Don't call your professors by their first name unless they tell you to do so.

Students sometimes believe that if their professors look young (not a problem in my case), that naturally it is all right to address them informally. But young professors especially have to establish a relationship of credibility and respect with their students. Such a relationship is necessary if the professor is going to teach and the student is going to learn.

Whether your teachers are young or old or in between, you should address them as "Professor Jones" or "Professor Smith."

What about calling your professor "Dr. Jones" or "Dr. Smith?"

Many university professors have Ph.D.s, and many of them refer to themselves as "Doctor." You can read it in their syllabus. I would still recommend that you address your teachers as "professor" and let them tell you if they would rather be called doctor or something else.

Some students call every faculty member "doctor" without knowing who has a Ph.D. and who doesn't. Professors who don't have a Ph.D. can either let it pass and have you call them "doctor" the whole semester, or they can correct you. Also, some professors with Ph.D.s don't want to be called doctor even though they could be addressed that way.

What to call your professors may seem trivial, but it is important for several reasons. Professors can be supportive and caring of their students, but the relationship has to have limits.

If not, students would be less likely to complete assignments when they are supposed to because they believe their "friend" the professor won't mind if the assignment is late. A good way to establish that the relationship is not casual or informal, and to show respect, is by calling professors by their last name, as in Professor Jones or Doctor Jones.

This is also good for you to learn early on. When you start looking for a job, you should know how to address people in the business world. Unless someone has told you that you don't call prospective employers by their first name, how will you know? You can learn this early on by addressing professors appropriately.

Going to class regularly

One of the best ways to lay the foundation for a good relationship with a professor is to go to class every day. There are other reasons, of course, why you want to attend each class, and some of them have been discussed in earlier chapters. But if the professor knows you are there all the time and sees you make a contribution to the class with comments or questions, the teacher is likely to notice you more than students who don't attend regularly or go the whole semester without saying anything.

Getting noticed in a class is much easier if there are 30 students as opposed to 100. If the class has a large number of students, you will have a tougher time getting the professor to remember who you are. But you never know when professors are going to be able to do something helpful for you, and they won't be able to do that unless they know your name and something about you. Even though it takes a greater effort to get to know a professor in a larger class, if that class is important, you should do what is necessary to establish a relationship with that professor.

You can overdo this. Sometimes, the same few students talk all the time in class. They constantly volunteer when the professor asks questions or raises issues to discuss. A professor may believe after a while that you are energetic in class because you want the maximum points for the "class participation" portion of the grade, or because you just want to be noticed.

One other way to get noticed by a professor in class is to make comments that show you have not only kept up with the reading, but have given the issues in the class some thought. Every teacher wants to see that. If you have some creative ways of looking at the course material, the professor is likely to remember your name and your comment.

**Get to know at least some of
your professors. Not enough students
do this and it is almost always worth the effort.**

Keeping in contact

Most classes meet two or three days a week. Fewer classes meet four or five days a week during the regular semester. If a professor is teaching an especially important course in your major, one that may lead to important connections when it comes to your career, you will need to keep in touch with the professor throughout the semester. Two or three days a week of seeing you in class, and hearing an occasional question or comment from you, may not be enough for the professor to remember you if that teacher has several hundred students in four classes that semester.

E-mail offers some advantages here. It gives you the chance to keep in contact with your professors without going to their office or talking to them after class.

The good thing about e-mail is how quick and easy it is to compose and send a message. That is also the downside of e-mail. Most professors get a lot of it. They constantly get messages from their students, colleagues, the department chair, the dean, and others from throughout the campus. It is not unusual for professors to have to answer 50 or more e-mails a day.

As a student, you should not send an e-mail to a professor just to say, "Enjoyed the lecture today. Keep up the good work." But if you want to ask a question, make a comment about something that was discussed in class or that you read in the book, or if you want to delight the professor by mentioning something you read that is beyond the requirements of the class, e-mail may be the best way to do it.

Try to keep your e-mail brief and avoid asking a lot of questions of your professor that would take too much time to answer. The best student e-mails are where you say to the professor something like, "I read that case you mentioned in class yesterday (that wasn't assigned). I thought the court was wrong when it decided. . ." The professor can read the note in seconds and write a quick response: "Dear Susan: Thanks for your note. I'm glad you found the case to be interesting. I agree that the court was shortsighted in its decision. . ." Although the professor's response was brief, he or she will likely remember that Susan e-mailed and that she read a case that was not assigned.

When an important guest speaker comes to the campus to talk to the faculty and a few students are invited to go to a lunch and meet that person, Susan is much more likely to be included than a student the professor doesn't know.

Going to office hours

Students should take advantage of professors' office hours. They are usually the four or more hours each week that a professor is supposed to be in the office and available to students. Sometimes, however, it doesn't work out.

Some professors consistently miss office hours without telling students in advance either in the classroom or by e-mail or in the class Web site, if there is one. They may be out of town attending a convention, or they may be giving an exam to a graduate student.

Sometimes you will show up for a professor's office hours and find a long line of students. If the professor has a class right after office hours and has to leave at a set time, he or she may not be able to see all the students. If that happens to you, e-mail with suggested times outside of office hours and get an appointment. Explain that you were there during the right time, but so were other students. Professors should always make time for you outside of office hours, but you should keep in mind the time constraints on a professor's schedule.

Not surprisingly, professors usually hold office hours when it is convenient for them, but not necessarily for the students. Professors who are early risers love to have office hours at 8 a.m. because they know hardly any students will bother them in their office the entire semester, and they will get a lot of work done during that period. You may have class during all the professor's office hours and would have to miss class to be able to go there during that time.

As a student, you should be assertive about insisting that the professor make an appointment outside of office hours if that is necessary. Professors know that students have other classes and have jobs that may prevent them from coming at certain times.

When you go to see a professor in the office, have something concrete to discuss. Professors often don't have time to just chat about things, although they will probably ask you a little about yourself and your career plans if they have not talked to you before. If you have a question about something in the textbook, or something in your lecture notes, bring those written materials with you. If you are unsure about the department's course requirements, bring a copy of the university bulletin so you can both see how the requirements are listed.

If you are seeing a professor because of an exam grade, you may want to drop the exam off in the professor's mailbox (make a copy for yourself first) before your visit so the professor can read it in advance. It will save time when you have your meeting.

Don't be easily offended

Some professors have an amazing ability to remember their students' names. There may be 50 or 100 students in the class, but within a few weeks, the professor knows your name and perhaps something about you. Other teachers are just not very good at remembering names.

If you have a professor in a large class, or you know the professor has three or four classes that semester, you should say your name when you talk to the professor the first few times. It is awkward for the professor, and for you, if you walk into the professor's office and start talking, yet the teacher can't remember your name. When you walk in, say "Hi, I'm Jill Robinson from your chemistry class. I wanted to talk to you about. . ." That way the professor can address you by your name.

If you suspect that a professor doesn't remember your name, don't be offended. Some students are sensitive about this. Their feelings may be hurt if they think they haven't gotten enough of their professors' attention so at least they remember your name. In fact, professors may remember quite a bit about you without always recalling your name instantly. After you and the professor have had several interactions, he or she will likely remember who you are.

Keeping in touch after graduation

The major you choose to study may have a direct connection to a career. In such programs, it is not unusual for employers to call professors to ask if they know of someone who could fill a position that has become available. They assume, often correctly, that a professor may know some qualified graduates or students about to graduate whom they can recommend.

If you have been keeping in touch with a few professors who are in a position to help you this way, your chances of being recommended are much greater than if you stopped communicating with your professors the moment you graduated. First, the professor will remember you because you will have e-mailed, written, or even telephoned once in a while to discuss how your career is going. If your last communication with your former professor wasn't very long ago, you may be one of the first people the professor thinks of when recommending someone for the job.

And second, the professor will know how to get in touch with you. Sometimes, when a student graduates, he or she will move away and can't be found easily. The alumni association, even if it offers free membership for the first year after graduation, may not know where to find you. If the professor knows about a job that would be terrific for you, they may try to reach your parents to see where you have moved, but that may require a lot of effort. Professors are more likely to recommend students they have heard from recently and know how to find.

Professors like to hear from their former students. They want to know how they are doing and what kind of success they are having in the field they are pursuing for which the professor helped them prepare. When former students are doing well, it gives professors much satisfaction.

Keeping in contact doesn't just help the student who graduated, it can help the students who are still in school. If you are going to be back on campus, let one of your former teachers know. You may be able to talk to a class and help those students better prepare for their careers.

Too few students keep in touch with their professors. They may call if they have a specific job situation or crisis and they need some immediate advice. But not very many keep in touch on a regular basis because they assume there is no advantage to them in doing so.

That can be shortsighted. On many occasions, a student whom I have not seen or heard from in many years will contact me to ask for a letter of recommendation for law school or graduate school. They have been working for a number of years and have decided to continue their education. They didn't ask for a letter before they graduated because they didn't expect to go back to school.

Sometimes I don't remember anything about them or even what they look like. If they got a good grade in the class, I usually agree to write the letter. But a letter of recommendation isn't much help when it says, "Bill got a "B" in my class. I don't remember anything about him, but if he got that grade, he must have been a good student."

You should communicate regularly with your former professors, especially those in the field directly related to your career. Even if that means just an occasional e-mail or letter, you should keep in touch.

E-mail is an especially effective way to keep in touch with your professors. You can write at some length about what you have been doing and how your career is going, while the professor can quickly respond.

You will also find that college will be more enjoyable if you get to know a few professors and talk to them outside of the classroom. By keeping in contact with them after you graduate, it may help you continue ties to the college and may lead to relationships that could make a difference to you later on.

What To Do When There Are Problems

There are times when a professor creates problems for one or more students, and someone has to say something to the professor. This can range from an annoying habit while the professor is lecturing, to not being clear when discussing the substantive material in the class.

Other problems may relate to language if it is difficult to understand a professor because of a heavy accent, or because the professor speaks so fast that students don't have time to take notes.

Some problems, such as when professors create an uncomfortable environment for their students, will be considered in a later chapter. This is a complicated and important issue that requires more detailed discussion.

Go see the professor first, if appropriate

Students are often reluctant to discuss a problem in the class with the professor. They assume, almost always incorrectly, that the professor will "retaliate" if you criticize or complain about the class or the professor's teaching.

What students may not realize is that professors often take great pride in their teaching method and ability. Whether they are just starting their academic careers or have been around a long time, almost every professor I have known *wants* to be a good teacher, even when he or she doesn't necessarily know how to do it.

Professors want to hear from students who have problems with the class even if that criticism is painful. Some professors know that students are hesitant to speak freely and they will give mid-semester evaluations so students can make anonymous and candid comments in writing and changes can be made before the semester ends.

Some student comments will be disheartening for the professor to read, especially if that person is trying hard to be a good teacher. For example, if a student says the class is boring and that the lectures are uninteresting or dry, that is not only unpleasant to hear, it is not something the professor can easily change. If, on the other hand, a student says the professor talks so fast it is hard for students to take notes, that is a problem that can be solved.

Although students may make candid comments on an evaluation form, few of them would tell a professor in person that something is wrong. Yet professors need to hear from students if there is a problem. You should make an appointment or go see the professor during office hours to discuss the matter rather than try to do it after class when other students may be nearby. Especially if there is something you are going to tell the professor that could be embarrassing, it is better done privately in the professor's office.

> *You should probably talk to the professor about these problems:*
> - You are having trouble following the course material in the lectures or the textbook.
> - The professor has annoying or distracting habits while lecturing that he or she may not be aware of and that could be corrected.
> - The professor talks so fast you have trouble taking notes.
> - The professor says things in class that make you uncomfortable or are offensive.
> - The professor does not make clear what is expected from you for the exams and papers.

When you tell the professor that you are not happy with some aspect of the course, his or her reaction may at first be defensive. That is probably a natural response to such criticism. No one wants to be known as a poor teacher. Therefore, when you say to the professor that he or she is not presenting the material in a way that can be understood by students, the professor may at first think you are not studying hard enough or paying attention or, although less likely, that you are not very smart and that brighter students must be getting what they need to out of the class.

Try to be specific when criticizing the professor or offering suggestions. If you make only general statements, a professor may not know what the problem is and how to fix the situation.

After the initial reaction, professors have a chance to think about what you said. Many times if the problem can be changed, the professor will do so. Any conscientious teacher will try to make appropriate changes after getting feedback from students.

One area that you should not complain about because the professor won't likely change it, and it may make you appear unmotivated, is if you say there is too much reading or too much work in the class. An experienced professor who has taught the class before has a pretty good idea how much reading and work should be assigned during the semester. The professor is not suddenly going to eliminate assignments because you think there is too much work in the class.

If, however, the professor sees this comment on the teaching evaluations over a period of several semesters, he or she may adjust the workload.

The teaching assistant

In some of your classes, in addition to the professor, there will be one or more teaching assistants. The duties of teaching assistants, who are usually graduate students, will vary, but most of them attend the lectures with you, then lead a "discussion" group one day a week. In many such situations, the teaching assistant will evaluate your work and assign your grade.

Students often find problems with teaching assistants. They may have trouble speaking English clearly, may not be experienced teachers or may not be familiar with the material in the class. If there is a problem, you should see the teaching assistant first. But if that is not likely to result in a change, then you should go see the professor.

Sometimes if students are unhappy about the professor's lectures or teaching style, they will feel more comfortable telling the teaching assistant, with the expectation that he or she will pass the information on to the professor without identifying the source.

You may need to see the department chair

Sometimes the nature of the problem with a professor requires you to talk to the department chair. Perhaps you believe that the professor makes inappropriate comments to students or creates an uncomfortable environment in the classroom. Depending on the situation, you may not be able to discuss those matters with the professor.

If it is serious, the department chair may consult with the provost or other high-level officials at the university. You may need to tell them the nature of the problem.

Be sure during each of your meetings with university officials that you are accurate about what the professor is doing wrong and if possible, bring documentary evidence to support the allegations. If other students can verify what you are saying, you may need to have them go with you.

Many universities have officials such as an ombudsperson or someone in the dean of students office who can give you advice on sensitive matters. You may want to talk to them before discussing the issue with the department chair.

You obviously won't have the same type of relationship with all your professors. For the professors who are teaching subjects that are especially important to you, make a sincere effort to get to know them. It will make your college experience more enjoyable and could make a difference in your career.

9

What Professors Do

Summary: This chapter describes the working environment for professors at various kinds of universities and the tenure system.

Why It Matters: *The better you understand what professors do and why, the more you will get from your college experience.*

One of the most difficult challenges all professors face is managing their time. They likely teach two, three, or four courses a semester with as many as several hundred students. They may have 50 to 100 advisees who get help with deciding which courses to take and with career plans.

Professors also spend many hours preparing lectures and exams, grading, meeting with students, and reading material to share with their classes. Depending on the type of university where they work, they may also spend a lot of time doing research and writing articles and books or pursuing creative activities.

Professors also have meetings throughout the semester. It is not unusual for professors to serve on half a dozen committees in addition to attending regular faculty meetings. They may be involved in short and long-range planning for their department. Depending on their field, they could meet with various constituent groups. For example, business professors often have continuing contact with local business leaders.

How busy your professors are and how they allocate their time make a significant difference to you as an undergraduate. The more you know about your professors' job environment, the better you will be able to interact with them.

Professors as Teachers

As a student, you may see a professor only in a classroom, and therefore it is understandable that you would believe that teaching is the only thing a professor does. However, that is not the case. Because professors are involved in so many activities, they may be limited in how much time they can spend with undergraduates.

It is difficult to make general statements about how professors spend their time because universities vary so much in their mission and what they expect of their faculty. But here are some issues to keep in mind:

Research universities

If you attend a four-year college that offers M.A. or Ph.D. programs, you are probably going to a research university. All of the "flagship" state universities such as University of Washington or University of California are research institutions. So are Harvard and Yale and other private universities.

Such institutions expect their professors to devote a significant portion of their time to doing research and publishing.

Depending on the professor's discipline, he or she may also be expected to apply for grants. All of those activities can take a lot of time.

In some fields, professors don't publish in traditional journals or write books. A history professor will write articles for scholarly journals or books, while an art or music professor is more likely to create works of art or compose music.

Professors at research universities teach fewer classes than their counterparts at "teaching" institutions. Many professors at research universities teach two or three courses a semester. In addition to undergraduate classes, they teach graduate seminars and are members of M.A. and Ph.D. committees. Supervising the work of students who are completing a graduate degree is often very time-consuming.

Teaching institutions

You may be attending or planning to enroll at an institution that is known as a "liberal arts" college. It may not have programs that offer an M.A. or Ph.D. Some of the most prestigious colleges in the country fit into this category.

Professors at these universities usually teach four or five classes a semester and may be involved in additional activities such as supervising student clubs or groups. Generally, professors at these institutions must be excellent teachers and they will be evaluated based on the quality of their teaching.

Some teaching colleges still expect faculty members to publish or undertake creative activities. So you can't assume that if you are at a non-research institution that your professor can devote almost all of his or her time to students.

This may be obvious but is worth stating: The more classes professors teach, the less time they will have for each student or each class or for research and publishing. If you have a professor who has a teaching load of five classes a semester, whether or not that person also does research, you may have a tough time getting to know that professor well.

Doing research requires time away from students

You may have a hard time finding your professor on campus. The reason could be that it is almost impossible for a professor to do research and writing at the office. Writing is difficult and requires a high level of concentration and long periods without being interrupted. At the office the phone rings constantly, students stop by to talk, a senior colleague wants to chat about an upcoming committee meeting, or 50 e-mails need to be answered. That is why many professors pick one or two days a week to work at home. They will often have e-mail there and can stay in touch that way, and they can check their voice mail at the office, but they have to be away from the university if they are going to do any writing. This can, of course, be frustrating for students who can't find their professors when they need them.

Nevertheless, professors who do research are often the best teachers. That is because they are able to discuss new and exciting developments in the field with their students.

Your professor's rank

You will read below about the tenure system, why it is so important to your professor, and how it affects you as an undergraduate. Before learning about tenure, it is helpful to see a list of ranks. Professors usually have one of the following titles. Knowing their rank may tell you a lot about how available they will be and what their job environment is like:

- Professor (also known as full professor)
- Associate professor
- Assistant professor
- Visiting assistant professor (or visiting associate or full professor)
- Acting assistant professor (or acting associate or full professor)

- Lecturer
- Adjunct professor

At most institutions, only the top two ranks (professor and associate professor) have tenure and are therefore likely to have a lifetime job at the university. This varies somewhat (an associate professor at some colleges may not have tenure) but is generally true. All other ranks do not guarantee permanent employment.

If your teacher is a professor or associate professor, it usually means he or she has been a faculty member for a long time and has a very strong publication and teaching record.

Your Professors' Tenure Status

Tenure is one of the most controversial aspects of higher education. Many people outside of universities (and some inside) don't understand why the system is necessary, and they may believe it protects professors who are not doing their jobs well.

The main feature of the tenure system is that it is *all or nothing*. When professors are awarded tenure, they will generally be able to stay at the university for their entire careers. Because no mandatory retirement age is in effect, some professors work at the same institution for 30 or 40 years.

If, on the other hand, a professor is rejected for tenure, he or she will be fired and must leave the university. There is no in between. A professor either is awarded what is almost always a lifetime position or is dismissed. Considering what is at stake, you can understand why professors consider this to be a very important matter.

The purpose of tenure

Tenure developed at colleges and universities in the 1920s and 1930s, although it was several decades after that before the protection that tenure presumably grants to professors became effective. Even today, some institutions of higher learning fail to honor the commitment they make to faculty members when they award tenure.

The purpose of tenure is to give faculty members protection against being fired arbitrarily. If they did not have such protection, they would not be able to help govern the university, challenge the policies of the university administration, undertake controversial research, and discuss sensitive topics in the classroom. That is why tenure is a *means* to an end. The "end" is the opportunity to speak and write freely, to take contentious positions on important issues, and to help run the university, without worrying about being fired unfairly.

A new professor

When a university hires a professor, that person is likely to hold the rank of assistant professor. Students sometimes get confused about this, thinking that because the word "assistant" is in the title, the person is not actually a professor, but instead simply "assists" professors. An assistant professor is almost always a full-time faculty member on what is called the "tenure track."

At most universities, when a professor earns tenure, he or she will be promoted to associate professor. This can be confusing because, as noted before, at some universities anyone with the rank of associate professor is tenured, while at others, some associate professors do not have tenure and will go through a tenure review.

You can tell quite a bit about your professors just by knowing their rank. An assistant professor will be facing a tenure judgment and will be trying to do what is necessary to obtain tenure. If your teacher is an associate professor, you can assume in most cases that he or she has successfully survived the tenure process and is assured of a permanent position at the university.

After an associate professor has been in that rank for a number of years and has developed a strong record in research and teaching, he or she may be promoted to full professor. Because they are tenured, associate and full professors can generally pursue research interests without worrying as much about how they will be perceived by the university. However, because many associate professors want to be promoted, they are sometimes reluctant to undertake controversial research projects or to be too outspoken on university issues.

Other ranks

All the other ranks are not tenure-track positions. Acting or visiting professors are not permanent members of the faculty and are likely teaching for only a year or two. Those professors often have a heavy teaching load.

A lecturer may be a member of the faculty, but such a position does not come with tenure. A lecturer will often have renewable contracts of one, two or three years, and can be terminated much more easily than a tenured professor. Lecturers almost always teach four classes or more a semester.

Adjunct professors usually teach part-time, often one course a semester, while continuing their regular job. Many adjuncts teach in the evening.

None of the professors in these positions—acting, visiting or adjunct—are expected to do research. In addition, they are likely to do less advising than regular professors and may not serve on committees.

Tenure Can Be Hard to Get

Because a university is making what is often a lifetime commitment to a faculty member, it wants to make sure that the standards for tenure are rigorous and applied fairly. That is difficult to do. Only so much of the process can be formalized and consistently applied. Personal relations and other factors may play significant roles in the tenure decision.

At many colleges and universities, tenure is very difficult to attain, and it is getting harder each year. The requirements for research and publishing are being increased at many institutions. At some universities, an assistant professor cannot hope to win tenure unless he or she has published a book *and* some additional work such as articles in scholarly journals. Not many years ago, publishing a few articles was enough.

How professors are reviewed

The probationary period for assistant professors is usually six years. During the sixth year, the professor is reviewed for tenure during a complicated, multi-stage process that usually lasts six to eight months. The first of several tenure committees will begin reviewing the professor's work early in the fall semester. The committee will evaluate the professor's teaching, research, and service to the university and community. After the tenure process moves from the department to the college committees and then a university-level review, the decision belongs to the president of the university or the institution's governing board.

Professors denied tenure at a college or university may never get another tenure-track job. They will be competing against 50-100 or more applicants for every position, and they will bear the stigma of having been denied tenure at another institution. The professor may be able to work part-time at a college for $2,000 or $3,000 per course, but the prospects of getting another tenure-track job are not great.

The probationary period is among the most stressful of a professor's life. The professor knows that during those years, he or she has to concentrate on those things that will count significantly in the tenure decision. At some universities, research and publications are much more important than teaching competence when it comes to tenure, so not surprisingly, there is substantial pressure on professors at those institutions to spend more time doing research and less time preparing for classes prior to the tenure review. At many universities, professors are expected to continue publishing after earning tenure.

What Matters for the Tenure Decision

For generally good reasons, how much professors publish is often the most important factor in determining whether they get tenure. This doesn't mean that teaching is not valued or is not considered a key issue in the tenure evaluation. At some colleges that pride themselves on being teaching institutions, how well a professor does in the classroom will be the most relevant consideration in the tenure decision. Even at universities where many faculty members do research and publish, the quality of teaching may be a key factor in close cases.

Teaching may count less because
it is hard to evaluate

A university can count how many articles and books a professor has published. When the administration wants the standards for tenure to be more rigorous, it can increase the number of publications required. (For some fields, how much grant money has been awarded to a professor is an important consideration). Such a system appears to set "objective" standards that can be applied to everyone going through the tenure process. There will obviously be disagreements about the quality of the research, but nevertheless, tenure and promotion committees can see how much was published.

Teaching, on the other hand, is very difficult to evaluate. Many factors make someone a good teacher. No easily measured standard exists.

Evaluations that students complete at the end of the semester provide important information, but students are not always the best judges of good teaching. Other professors can sit in on classes but they almost always announce they are coming. Thus, a visitor may not see what the professor's teaching is like on an average day.

Universities say that teaching is important. But in reality, because teaching is hard to measure and because the reputation of the university usually depends more on research than on teaching, it is not surprising that research activity is such an important part of the tenure evaluation.

Assistant professors look for clues from senior colleagues that tell them what really counts. They are likely to hear this advice about teaching:

- At teaching institutions, the quality of teaching will be the most significant factor in the tenure decision.
- At colleges and universities where professors are expected to do research, a professor with a lot of publications, but an uninspired teaching record, is likely to get tenure. A professor with a mediocre publication record, and outstanding teaching, is likely not to get tenure.

Professors are also expected to perform service functions. That means they serve on various committees within the university and are active in off-campus activities that relate to the work of the department. While all universities consider service as part of the tenure review, some value it more highly than others. Generally, the more a professor is expected to publish, the less he or she will be expected to perform service duties.

What This Means for You

No matter how busy they are, you are entitled to have professors who are committed to teaching and their students.

Even if they are under a lot of stress because they are facing a tenure review, or they are involved in a research project, professors have an obligation to be well prepared for each class and to be pleasant to you and other students. But you should also recognize how much demand there is for your professors' time and how their non-teaching activities can contribute positively to your education.

The emphasis on research helps undergraduates

You and your parents may wonder why research is so important, and why good teachers who inspire students are sometimes forced to leave a university after six years.

To explain this briefly, it really does make sense for many colleges and universities to emphasize research when making tenure decisions. Almost everyone associated with a university understands the importance of good teaching, and even leading research institutions have made an effort in recent years to improve the quality of undergraduate instruction. But research is often the main reason why a professor does or does not earn tenure.

You need to be taught by professors who are both *reading* extensively in the field, and thus keeping up with new developments, and *publishing*. A professor who has stopped learning, and who delivers lectures from the same stale notes that he or she has been using for years, is not serving the students well.

Professors have an obligation to be knowledgeable about the work of researchers in their subject who make new discoveries, develop new theories, and discuss cutting-edge issues, and to share that information with their students.

But it often takes more to keep abreast of developments in the field than simply reading books or articles that others have written. When professors conduct research *themselves* and publish the results of their work, they can discuss exciting developments with their students, and do so with enthusiasm. They are also likely to know more about a particular issue than almost anyone and, depending on the nature of the research, may be contributing significantly to the improvement of peoples' lives.

Research and teaching often go together. It is not unusual for professors who are the most active researchers to be among the best teachers.

It is not very stimulating for students when their professors teach the same courses semester after semester, year after year, if the material they cover doesn't change to reflect up-to-date information or what the professor has learned by doing research. Being able to share newly discovered knowledge with students helps professors to maintain an interest in the field and passion for teaching over an extended period of time.

The university's reputation and the value of your diploma

Colleges and universities do not generally become prestigious based on the quality of their teaching. Some liberal arts colleges are known for having small classes, gifted teachers, and good equipment such as computers, and over time, can acquire a reputation as a great place for undergraduate instruction. But usually, what takes place in a classroom, even if the teaching is outstanding, does not get widely disseminated.

A college or university ordinarily becomes well known because its professors write articles and books and other publications, or undertake creative work. The publications are read and discussed by other professors, professionals in the field, and sometimes the general public. Creative accomplishments of the faculty can be made available to both academic communities and the public. When a university enjoys a reputation for doing innovative research or creative work, it becomes better known. That, in turn, can make your diploma more valuable.

The "prestige" of a university is difficult to measure and can be over-emphasized. But if you graduate from an institution that is recognized for its research, you have likely benefited from having professors who share the results of that research with their students. Prospective employers and graduate admissions committees know that.

It is important to stress that you can get a first-rate undergraduate education at an institution where professors don't do research. Many colleges and universities have dedicated teachers who do not publish. However, when it comes to a university's reputation and how that reputation enhances the value of your diploma, research achievements are more likely to be widely known than accomplishments in the classroom.

Recognize the demands
on your professors' time

Ask your professor or someone in the department about your professor's rank and tenure status. Be understanding if your professor is going through an especially stressful and demanding period. If he or she is an assistant professor facing a tenure decision within a year or two, the time demands may be overwhelming. As mentioned before, even tenured professors may be busy with research, other classes, and committee work.

You don't have to be apologetic about asking for your professors' time and attention. Being available to students is part of their job. But it is helpful for you to understand that there are times when a professor will be less accessible or will have limited time to spend with you. Knowing a little about your professors' work environment will help you learn how best to interact with them and get the most out of your relationship.

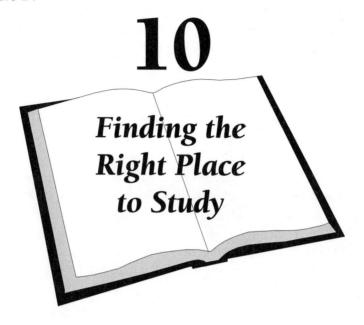

Part IV

10

Finding the Right Place to Study

Summary: This chapter recommends some things to consider when trying to find a good place to study.

Why It Matters: It is not always easy to find somewhere to study that is both quiet and comfortable. Some advance planning may help.

If you are in your senior year of high school and going away to college in the fall, you may not have any choice but to live in the dorms your first year. University administrators want students to live on campus their freshman year because they believe it helps you to get used to college life faster, to meet friends, to get higher grades, and to avoid the problems associated with finding an off-campus place to live.

Besides requiring you to live in the dorm, the university will most likely choose your roommates for the first year. It may not be until your sophomore year when you can pick those you want to live with and to move off campus into an apartment or house.

You will be doing hours of homework every semester and you will soon learn, if you don't know already, how important it is to find the right environment in which to study. It is often harder than you think.

Managing your time will be among your biggest challenges when you go to college. There will be classes to attend, homework, social events, volunteer activities, perhaps a part-time job and maybe an internship, and other things to do. When you devote the hours to studying that you have set aside for that purpose, you have to use that time efficiently. If not, you will either study for more hours than is necessary, or if you don't have the additional time, you may learn less in your classes than you would otherwise and your grades may suffer.

It is also important that you have long stretches of time when you can study without being interrupted. You will be a more successful student if you can concentrate on a subject for an extended period of time, rather than study in a series of short spurts. As you get busier, you may find that it is difficult to set aside enough time to study without being disturbed or distracted.

It May Be Hard To Study in the Dorms

Unless you are one of those lucky people who is able to shut out noise and concentrate on what you are reading or writing no matter what is going on around you, you are likely to find it difficult to study in the dorms. Two or three of you may be living in a small room, and it will be very hard for you to concentrate with three people studying at the same time even if everyone is relatively quiet. Sometimes people make annoying sounds inadvertently. Sometimes the temptation to talk is too great, and you end up not using your time for studying wisely.

It seems as if it is rarely quiet in a dorm. You may be fortunate enough to live in one with strict rules about noise. Some dorms have whole floors or study areas where rules about noise are strictly enforced. But some dorms that have set hours that are supposed to be for studying don't take those restrictions seriously. Most likely there will be times when you want to study but can't because you hear music or voices from next door or down the hall. The bass sounds from stereos may be especially distracting.

Dorm "quiet" rooms

You should check to see if your dorm has study or quiet rooms that have comfortable places to study. In some dorms, the "study" room consists of little more than a few tables and straight-back chairs. Such a study room environment may be uncomfortable, but it is close to your dorm room and you can take a quick break without having to go too far.

Depending on where the rooms are of students who socialize many days a week, even the lounge or separate study room may not be good for doing homework. Often the study room is located between or right next to dorm rooms, so you can hear whatever noise comes from those rooms while you are trying to concentrate. The lounge may be noisy if many students are trying to use it, or if there are a lot of people just passing through.

Finding a comfortable and quiet place to study is not always easy to do but is very important.

---

*The library is better,
but not ideal*

Because it may be difficult to find somewhere in the dorm to study, many students seek refuge in the library. Although the library will generally be quieter than the dorm and you probably can find someplace to be by yourself, there are places in the library where you may have to study that are so uncomfortable that students don't like to spend too many hours there.

In the library, there are probably some soft chairs in a quiet place where you can sit for hours and concentrate. But if the library is crowded that night, or if you have a lot of writing to do, you may end up at a study cubicle with nothing more than a desk and hard chair.

Because it is the library you are not supposed to have anything to eat or drink with you. If you want to get something or use the bathroom, you need to take all of your stuff or risk having it stolen. If you take everything with you, there is a chance that someone will be in your spot when you get back. That is one reason why you may want to study with a friend.

There is also a serious matter related to safety. Some old libraries have places that get almost no foot traffic. The advantage is that no one will likely bother you in that obscure section of the building. But if someone wanted to rob you or something worse, you would be isolated and vulnerable.

Then there is the walk back to the dorm. If you study in the library until late at night, you will be leaving in the dark and there may be few people around. Some university campuses are poorly lighted even near the library where students come and go at night. At many universities, students leaving the library late at night have been robbed.

Some colleges offer student patrols where you can call a phone number before you leave the library, and someone will escort you to your dorm room or car. But you may think you don't need the service or that it is too much trouble to call. On busy nights, you may have to wait a while before someone will meet you.

Being concerned about your safety makes a lot of sense. Students should take steps to reduce the chances they will be a crime victim while at college. Being careful when you leave the library late at night and walk through the campus is one of the most important things you can do.

If you have been studying with friends or know they will be out at a certain time, you may be able to meet them so you can walk home together. Arranging a time and place in advance is worth the effort.

Another quiet place to study may also be the local public library or a friend's place if that person lives in a quieter environment. If you want to get away to study for exams and you can afford it, you may want to rent a hotel room for a night or two.

Moving Off Campus

During your second semester, if the university allows it, or at the beginning of your sophomore year, you may want to move off campus. If you can afford it, you may want to consider living by yourself in an apartment fairly close to campus. That way you won't have to worry about finding a quiet and comfortable place to study unless your neighbors are noisy.

But many students, either due to financial reasons or the desire to live with friends, move into a house or apartment with several other students. Sometimes that works out well, but other times, it may be hard to study there. If it is a house with four or five roommates, the odds are good that one of the residents will have a visitor, or is playing music, or is watching television, or is doing something else that is noisy at any given time. You may be paying a lot of money to rent a room in an apartment or house near campus, but you may not want to spend much time there.

Choose your roommates carefully

Although it is often a lot of fun to live with your friends, think carefully before moving in with someone who isn't as serious about school or doesn't study as much as you do. When you are deciding to move in with people you already know or are interviewing prospective roommates whom you have never met, there is no easy way to find out if they will be considerate when you want to study. Although it is not a job interview, ask them about their study and personal habits. Find out as much as you can about their routine, whether they want the apartment or house to be quiet when it is time to do homework, or if they like to blast the television or stereo from the moment they get home from class.

If you move in with the wrong people, you could be stuck with them for a full academic year. The landlord is not going to let you out of the lease unless you find someone else to take your place, and you won't be able to do that once the semester starts because almost everyone will be committed elsewhere. I have known students who were sorry they allowed a friend of a friend to move into the apartment or house because that person created an impossible situation that made everyone miserable. A surprising number of students have told me they spend as little time as they can in their apartment or house either because it is too noisy to study or they can't stand one of their roommates. When there is constant tension because of the living situation, it is hard to concentrate on your studies and enjoy college.

Watch out for the neighbors

You and your friends have found a great house off campus. It's two blocks from the edge of the university. Although your room is expensive, the house is in relatively good shape and there is more than one bathroom. You have also done a great job choosing your roommates. Everyone who will live in the house knows when it is time to study.

But then you find out that each of the houses around you has five or six students living in them, and they are anything but quiet neighbors. The houses are close enough together so you can hear their music, their parties, and their voices almost anytime of the night. You have signed a lease and are stuck.

There may not be much you can do about the situation. Try to reason with your neighbors to see if they will lower the music or control their party guests. However, if you talk to them about keeping down the noise, they may say that you knew what you were getting into when you moved into a neighborhood close to campus. If you call the police because the noise is unbearable, your neighbors may discover you were the source of the complaint and may retaliate. And as long as it is off campus, there is most likely nothing the university administration can do to help.

It is not enough to pick good roommates for your off-campus apartment or house. You have to make sure that you are living in a neighborhood that will allow you to study when you want to. Many students, who think that by moving off campus they will have a living environment that is better for serious work, learn this lesson only after it is too late. They are then stuck in that situation for a year or more. That means one year of the four you spend as an undergraduate was much less enjoyable than it should have been.

What You and Your Parents Should Do

There is no easy solution. Almost any dorm room, apartment or house could be potentially so noisy that you have a difficult time studying and sometimes sleeping. Even if you want to have your own place and you or your parents spend the extra money so you can live by yourself, there is no guarantee that it will be quiet there.

The only way to increase the odds that you will find the right place to live is to check things out as carefully as you can in advance. Don't agree to let people move into your apartment or house until you have met them and talked to them for a while. Don't agree to it just because someone you know recommends that person and you are nervous about finding an additional roommate to share the rent and utilities.

Before you decide on an off-campus house, walk through the neighborhood on a weeknight at 10 p.m. and imagine what it would be like to study under those conditions. Or check it out on a weekend evening to see if you would be able to sleep. Ask some older residents what it is like to live in that neighborhood. They may have a lot to tell you if they have been putting up with the noise for a long time.

Socializing, meeting and spending time with friends, going to parties, and yes, making a lot of noise once in a while are all part of the college experience. But as you spend more time at a university, you will likely appreciate how important the years as an undergraduate are and how quickly they go by. If you are trying to get the most you can out of your college experience, you must have a comfortable, safe and quiet place to study. Planning ahead and asking the right questions may make a big difference.

11

Extra-Curricular Activities

Summary: This chapter explains why you should become involved in activities outside of class.

Why It Matters: College will be a much more enriching experience if you participate in extra-curricular activities, especially if they are connected to your studies.

One of the great pleasures of being in college is the chance to be involved with one or more of the many groups and organizations associated with the campus. Not only will you almost always learn a lot through such activities, including things about yourself, you will meet people who may become longtime friends or contacts for your career. Depending on the nature of the group or organization, you may also be able to improve the lives of others through your work. Students who appreciate being at a university often say they want to "give something back," and that is one reason so many are involved in such activities.

If you do little more than go to class and do homework, you will miss out on much of what college has to offer. You may also be somewhat less appealing to a graduate or professional school, or a prospective employer. They want interesting, well-rounded students.

One of the biggest challenges related to extra-curricular activities, but one with potentially the biggest payoff, is trying to connect your outside endeavors with your class work. When you are able to do that, you will reap personal and professional rewards that you would otherwise not likely enjoy.

An Almost Endless Variety of Things To Do

A college or university will offer you the chance to be involved with a lot of different groups and organizations. Some are sponsored by the student government association and receive funds from it. Some clubs or groups form around the religious, racial, or ethnic background of students who want to get to know people of similar origins and interests, and to persuade the larger university community of the importance of their group identities. They will often hold meetings, sponsor events, invite speakers from on or off campus, and provide emotional support and encouragement to their members.

Other groups, such as those associated with political parties or environmental causes, try to interest students in public affairs. They often want to persuade the university to recognize their views on important issues and to impact elections in the city and state in which the college is located.

Others involve the arts including music, dance, and theater. Participation in such activities may not lead to a lifelong career, but they are likely to be enjoyable and something you will remember for a long time. For some students, taking part in such groups is one of the most gratifying things about being in college.

Social groups, such as sororities and fraternities, also provide an opportunity to participate in a variety of activities and to make friends and contacts who may be important for your career.

Making the connection

Some students pursue majors that permit an easy link between their academic work and outside activities. If you are a music major with an emphasis on vocal performance and you join the university chorale group, you are able to "practice" in the real world what you are learning in the classroom. Your studies and your work in the chorale group will complement each other.

If you are a political science major, the opportunities to make a connection between school and outside activities are almost endless. You can work for a candidate who is running for city council, state legislature or Congress. You can volunteer at an organization that lobbies to protect open space from development. You can do an internhip at a state or federal agency and see what real politics looks like up close. If you think you are headed for law school, you can work with a group that provides legal services to the poor. What you study in the class will seem relevant and exciting rather than disconnected from your primary interests.

If you are a computer science major, you can join a club that encourages its members to compare new developments in software and hardware, to experiment with cutting-edge technology, and to get to know others on campus with similar interests.

If you are an English major interested primarily in poetry, you can join a group of students who may publish a book of poems or create a Web site that features their work.

There are many more examples like this. Be creative and energetic in finding outside activities that relate to what you are learning in the classroom. It will make college more than just a series of classes, exams, and research papers.

Balancing your time

One of the most difficult challenges you will face in college is budgeting your time. You will have to make decisions about how much time to spend on your homework and how much to spend on outside activities. If you have to work at a job more than 15 hours a week, it will be even harder to find enough time to do all the things that interest you.

The activities you pursue outside of the classroom may be some of the most enjoyable and important time you spend while a student. You can more easily justify the additional time spent on the non-classroom work if you can make a connection to your academic pursuits, but you will never have enough time to do all the things you want.

In some cases, your extra-curricular activities will help you use what you learn in class in real world situations. That may make you understand better what you are learning and may improve your grades.

Many students successfully juggle their activities so they are able to join campus groups without it negatively affecting their grades. You have to decide whether your membership in an on-campus or off-campus organization is a worthwhile use of your time. But unless you also have to work many hours a week, you should not worry that a reasonable amount of time

---

Learn about extra-curricular activities from the campus newspaper, student government office, the university student affairs office, your dorm resident adviser, your academic adviser, or a professor.

spent doing interesting activities will detract from your college experience. It will, most likely, have the opposite effect of making your time in college much more meaningful.

Those who don't participate may feel a sense of isolation

Sometimes students feel isolated and lonely at college. Probably quite a few students experience these feelings in the first semester or two while they are meeting people and trying to make friends, but the situation often gets better as you begin your sophomore year.

But for some students, it doesn't get easier. You will "meet" dozens of students in your classes, but it is often difficult to get to know them even though you are in the same room several days a week for months. Usually, there is not much time for visiting before or after class.

For students who may feel disconnected from the campus or other students, a possible solution is to become involved in one or more organizations. You are likely to meet students with similar interests. By working on projects with others, you may have the chance to interact with them in a relaxed setting. That may help you gain self-confidence, and it may lead to new friendships.

Students who feel isolated at a college campus may not be able to concentrate as well on class work as students who are involved in campus activities. That may seem like an odd statement because, presumably, the student who is not doing much besides going to class and doing homework would have fewer distractions. But how much you study and get out of your courses may have a lot to do with how you feel about yourself and your college experience. It is better to spend at least some time on activities that make you feel connected to the campus.

A recent study by a Harvard professor clearly demonstrates that if students are involved in non-classroom activities and they can relate them to what they are studying, they will be much happier and more fulfilled as students, and they will get much more out of their college experience. (Richard J. Light, *Making the Most of College: Students Speak Their Minds,* Harvard University Press, 2001).

Student Media

Perhaps it comes as no surprise that I would enthusiastically recommend that students become involved with media organizations. What may be unexpected is that I believe students should work with the campus media regardless of their major and career interests.

The campus newspaper

Almost every college or university has a student newspaper. Sometimes the newspaper is part of the journalism program and is thus not "independent" of the university. Other times, the student newspaper occupies offices on campus and receives free rent and utilities from the university but is considered independent. In such a circumstance, a publication board may be in charge. Such a board often has professors and staff from the college on it, but the newspaper itself is not part of the university.

It goes without saying that every student interested in journalism, whether print or broadcast, should work for the school newspaper. But students from other majors should as well.

First, by developing story ideas, covering news events, and writing stories, you will meet some of the most important and interesting people on campus. As an ordinary student, you would probably never be able to ask the president of the university questions in a one-on-one interview or at a press conference. You will interview professors about their research and university administrators about important issues and events on campus. Just meeting these people and developing the ability to ask them questions will help you gain self-confidence and make your college years more interesting.

You will also be able to cover fun and interesting news events. You may get a courtside pass to the basketball game and a chance to interview players in the locker room. You may have the opportunity to see a robot being tested in a computer lab or attend a fraternity or sorority charitable event.

Second, your work on the school paper will help you develop writing skills. Previously in this book, I have discussed how important it is to develop writing skills while in college and how hard it is to do that. Whether you are working as a reporter or one of the editors who reviews reporters' stories, you will enhance your writing ability.

Third, you will be making an important contribution to the university and the surrounding community. It is essential that the student newspaper provide fair and thorough coverage of important issues and events on and off campus. How well a university functions and how it is perceived by the outside world depend to some extent on how well campus constituencies can exchange information and be informed about important issues. Students, staff and faculty, and those who live near the university, depend on the campus newspaper to provide much of that information.

Fourth, a student newspaper must reflect the diversity of the campus. That is why it is important for students from different majors and different racial, ethnic and cultural backgrounds to contribute to the newspaper's news and opinion pages. Although journalism students will usually take quite a few courses outside of their major and may become knowledgeable in certain fields, they will never have the same interest in some subjects as students majoring in those fields. The quality of the newspaper depends to some extent on the expertise of those who write for it.

Student radio station

Most universities have a radio station that is largely run by students. The stations are often licensed by the Federal Communications Commission and can be heard within a reasonable distance of the campus.

If you are interested in music or in broadcast news, you should consider working at the radio station. The radio station staff is not usually as well organized as the campus newspaper, and there may be limited opportunities to conduct interviews and prepare news broadcasts, but you will learn a lot and often enjoy the experience of sharing your interests with the audience. As noted above with the campus newspaper, students from diverse backgrounds should get involved in the campus radio station.

Many colleges have "professional" radio stations that broadcast at enough power to be heard many miles from campus and that employ mostly professional staffs. But there are likely to be part-time jobs or internships available that may be interesting and fun and provide good experience.

The yearbook

If you are interested in photography or in layout, you may find the yearbook to be an interesting experience. It is probably published once a year, and thus much of the work may be concentrated within a few months. That could create problems if you have a heavy course load that semester. But especially for those who want to see their photographs published, it may be worthwhile to join the yearbook staff.

Sororities and Fraternities

At many college campuses, students belong to a sorority or fraternity, and involvement with one of those organizations is immensely important to them. You can get to know quite a few students that way, form lifelong friendships, some of which may help your career, and have the chance to participate in many worthwhile charitable events. You will also likely be invited to parties and participate in other activities.

It is beyond the scope of this book to discuss sororities and fraternities at length. But a few things about such organizations should be mentioned here.

First, being part of the Greek system can take a lot of your time. If you live in a sorority or fraternity house, you may be tempted to spend too many hours socializing and doing things that don't always seem directly related to your primary purpose of being in college. Some houses impose strict rules about study hours and encourage students to do well academically, but others are centered more on socializing and partying than on academics.

Second, they can be somewhat confining in the sense that students with similar backgrounds often belong to the same sorority and fraternity. One of the most important things about college is to learn from the experiences of people of different racial, ethnic and cultural identities. Students who had little contact with people of diverse backgrounds when they were growing up benefit greatly by getting to know people who are different from themselves while in college.

And third, sororities and fraternities sponsor a lot of charitable events. Besides the social connections you may make, the charitable work you do with your sorority and fraternity may be among the most satisfying activities you undertake with them. You will learn to organize and publicize events, to raise money, and to know how it feels to do something good for people who are less fortunate.

Check Things Out First

Before you join a club or group, or a political organization, or a sorority or fraternity, talk to those who have been involved. Find out the benefits of being a member, how you will likely spend your time, and what you will get out of it.

Not everything that initially looks interesting and fun turns out that way. By asking questions of the right people in advance, you will be in a better position to know which organizations will be best for you and will make your college experience more enjoyable and worthwhile.

12

Having an Impact on Your School

Summary: This chapter encourages you to think about how you can contribute to your college or university as a student and after you graduate.

Why It Matters: Colleges and universities need active, engaged students and supportive alumni.

This book has discussed how your college or university will change you. During your undergraduate years, you will mature socially and intellectually. You will meet a variety of people, discover an interest in new subjects, make decisions about a career, and, if you have taken full advantage of being a student, you will have learned things that will make a difference in how you live your life.

While you are a student, you should think about not just how your college is having an impact on you, but how you can have an impact on your school. Colleges and universities need students who care about the institution and want to see it improve. You can help the university get better in numerous ways and in the process, enhance its reputation and the value of your diploma.

Volunteer for Department Committees

Students are in a special position to know what is working well when it comes to their courses and the curriculum they must complete for their majors. The faculty and administration ultimately make the decisions about what courses should be offered and what should be taught in those courses. But they should consult with students about those matters so professors can offer the courses that will provide the best educational experience.

Some university departments invite students to serve on established committees that meet regularly. Those committees often deal with curriculum issues, the department's budget and physical facilities, technology such as computers and video equipment, and relationships with alumni and professional organizations. Sometimes students meet occasionally with the department chair or other members of the faculty to talk about mutual interests and concerns. Some students represent student organizations within the department on either established or ad-hoc committees.

If your school or department does not have a formal process for involving students, you and some of your classmates should make an appointment with the chair. You should explain that student views should be represented when faculty members make important decisions and that you are volunteering to serve on a committee or to meet regularly with the department head or a group of faculty members. It is possible that the department chair had not given much thought to the idea of student participation and would respond positively to your suggestion.

The hiring of faculty

Among the most important decisions that any university faculty makes is the hiring of new professors. The individuals the department selects may be with the university for 30 years or more if they earn tenure. Because professors can only be experts in a few areas, the decision as to which of the many applicants to hire may affect for many years what kinds of courses will be offered and the direction of the department. Less visible to the students, but nevertheless also important, is what kind of research the new faculty member will do.

Ask the department chair if the faculty will be hiring any new professors. If they are, volunteer to serve on the search committee. The committee will write a job ad, decide where to advertise the position, review applications, select applicants to be interviewed, and make a recommendation to the department chair and faculty. Meeting regularly with the search committee and reviewing the application materials may require a lot of time, but you will be representing your fellow students in a process that is extremely important.

Even if students are not permitted to serve on the search committee, you should meet with the candidates when they come to campus to be interviewed. Those visits usually take place early in the spring semester. After you have met with the candidates, you can make your views known to the faculty by writing a brief report on your impressions of the applicants and giving it to the department chair. Almost every department head and faculty member will appreciate your participation and will consider your comments when making a decision. Your views will be more influential if you met with all the candidates who came to the school and can compare them.

You may have to be assertive about asking for time with the person being interviewed. Candidates are often on campus for one day. They have to meet with individual professors, the department chair, the dean, and other university administrators. They may also talk to representatives of constituent groups, such as professionals who work in the field. The candidate's schedule is often very tight. Despite that, request that you and other students get at least half an hour alone with the candidate to talk candidly about the program and his or her background.

Other committees

From time to time, professors revise the department's curriculum. This is an ideal opportunity for you to be involved in a meaningful way in shaping the future of the program.

Ask to be appointed to one of the committees that is going to recommend to the full faculty what courses should be offered and what the major requirements should be. You may have to be assertive with the department chair and the faculty because they may not have thought about consulting with students. But changing the curriculum is very important. With various levels of the university having to give their approval, it can easily take a year or more to revise the curriculum. Changes are not made very often; thus the new course of study must reflect and anticipate the changing nature of the field.

When faculty revise the curriculum, they have to make decisions about what courses there will be and when they will be offered. If you are a senior and have taken most of the classes you need for your degree, you will be able to contribute a lot to the discussion. Professors should seek student input before making these important changes.

Student organizations within the department

Many departments have student organizations or clubs. They try to get students to attend meetings, hear guest speakers, and meet informally with faculty. Some student groups are affiliated with national organizations and charge dues. That money will buy you membership in the local and national group and may give you a subscription to the organization's magazine.

You should belong to such student groups. You will get to talk outside of class with fellow students and guest speakers about issues of mutual interest, and you will likely have an opportunity to meet with the department chair or members of the faculty to discuss issues of importance to the students. You will also be able to attend conventions where you may meet a future employer.

Student Government

Participating in student government can be exciting and fulfilling. Student officers and the student senate make decisions as to which groups will be funded when they allocate money from student fees. They can also bring needed attention to important issues that affect the university.

You could be involved either as a member of the student legislative body or one of the officers. Try to work on something that can be accomplished during the year you are serving in that office. Cooperate with university officials who are in a position to actually make changes. You may be surprised to see how open they are to working with you on issues that affect students. People who work at universities are almost always there because they have a commitment to education and to students. They want to improve things, but they may need student support for those changes.

Student Activism

In recent years, there has been an increase in political activism on some campuses. Students have protested their university's involvement with companies that market products made in sweatshops and under conditions that are close to slave labor. They have taken over administration building offices to protest the way a university compensates its lowest-paid employees. Students have protested other policies of government or their university and have sometimes been successful in opening a dialogue with university officials about those issues.

You should consider it your right and even your responsibility to become involved in such matters. However, you must find a way to make your views known without breaking any laws. By taking over offices, vandalizing property, or committing other illegal acts, you not only lose public support for your cause, you also run the risk of having an arrest and conviction on your record. That could create problems for you later when you apply for a job.

After You Graduate

You should keep in touch with at least a few of your professors after you graduate. As mentioned in a previous chapter, they may be in a position to help by recommending you for a job or in other ways.

You should also keep in contact with them because there are things you can do to help your university and department. As you gain experience in your field, and if you are ever near the campus, offer to speak to a class. Students need to know what it is like in the "real" world and to be inspired by those working in the career they want to pursue.

Many departments have advisory boards made up of professionals in the field. Some are graduates of the program and have a special attachment to it. Those boards will meet once a month or every few months with the department chair or the faculty to discuss what is going on in the department, what plans the faculty have for the future, and what changes should be made.

If you serve on such a board, you will soon see that you were chosen not only for your career experience and your affection for the department but also because you may contribute money to the program or know people who could.

There is nothing wrong with that. Almost all colleges, whether public or private, need money from alumni for scholarships, the upgrading of labs, computers, video equipment, and many other things.

If you are serving on an advisory board, ask how you can help. If you are making a good salary, contribute to the scholarship fund so students with financial need can work fewer hours at a job and concentrate more on school. If you know people in your industry who may be interested in helping to buy equipment or something else the department needs, give that person's name to the development office. If the development staff wants you to go to lunch with the potential donor, agree to do that.

Even if you live far from the campus, you should join the alumni association so you will receive the monthly or quarterly magazine. Make sure the department where you majored has your current address so it can send you its newsletter by regular mail or e-mail. It will help you feel as if you are still part of the university.

When you are a high school senior or a freshman or sophomore in college, these things may seem a long way off. But you should make your college experience last well beyond the day you receive your diploma. Remaining interested in your college or university, and active in the department, is one of the best ways to do that.

Part V

13

Dealing with an Uncomfortable Environment

Summary: This chapter discusses potential problems in the professor/student relationship.

Why It Matters: Students need to know how to deal with certain troublesome situations.

Professors and university administrators must create the right kind of environment for learning. Professors will see you in classes, in their offices, and sometimes other places. In each setting, they need to treat you appropriately. Some rules are clear, and professors know that certain kinds of behavior will not be tolerated by the university, but at other times it is not obvious where the lines should be drawn. Those situations can make you feel uncomfortable.

The relationship between you and your professors should be relatively simple. Professors want you to learn and to be excited about the course material. They may take a personal interest in how you are doing in the class and how well you are preparing for your career.

But sometimes it gets more complicated.

At the same time that your teachers encourage you to do well, they are judging the quality of your work. You and your professors should recognize that those roles are distinct. You may not understand why a professor who has been supportive and encouraging can be judgmental or demanding when it comes to evaluating your work and assigning grades. Professors sometimes don't realize that in trying to help you with the class or with career issues, they do or say things that make you uneasy.

Professors will interact with you differently depending on the circumstances. In the classroom, professors will likely be careful what they say to avoid causing embarrassment. In their office, professors can be more candid about your work and your potential.

The Classroom

You should be able to sit in a classroom and ask questions or make comments without professors saying things that embarrass you. At the same time, you should not be so sensitive to criticism that you ignore the advice or suggestions they offer.

Professors should always be careful how they treat you in front of your classmates. When calling on you, it is easy for a professor to say something that will make you feel awkward. For example, if you ask a question on a topic that had just been covered in the lecture, a professor may be tempted to say, "If you had been paying attention, you would know. . ." A teacher should avoid doing that. It is possible that you were paying attention and didn't understand the material the first time it was presented. Even if annoyed by the question, the professor should just answer it without making the negative comment.

Professors should not make you feel incompetent or unprepared for university work. Thus, a teacher should not respond to a question by asking, "How did you get here? This is college, not high school."

There is almost always a nice way for professors to answer a question that appears to show that you are not doing the reading or paying attention carefully in class. If you ask something that was clearly covered in the reading assigned for that day, the professor can pick up the textbook and point out the page number and perhaps read a passage. Professors should not say something like, "If you would bother to do the reading, you would know not to ask me that question."

But beyond some of these obvious examples, it gets more complicated. Professors must demand a high level of commitment from students. They want you to do all the reading, pay close attention to the lectures, study hard for exams, and do a good job with research papers. Professors should push you to work hard and to stretch your mind to learn new and complex concepts.

There may come a point, however, when a professor is not offering useful advice but is instead so critical, that you feel uncomfortable interacting with the professor. If that happens, you may want to say something to the professor or, if it is more serious, the department chair.

Try to get the matter resolved. Your relationship with that professor may be too important for your college work or career to let a single conversation or interaction spoil it.

If something bothers you and you don't want to talk to the professor about it, or it is not serious enough to bring to the attention of the department chair, you may want to see the university's ombudsperson. Many universities have such a staff or faculty person on campus. They are trained to listen to your concerns and make suggestions. They will keep your comments confidential if you so request, or if you want, they will talk to the professor about your complaint. It can be a relatively easy way to settle the matter without you having to go to the head of the department.

When teachers make negative comments on your exams or research papers, or characterize your in-class comment as inadequate, they are trying to help you learn. You should not take it personally because it is rarely meant to be personal. It is part of the normal interaction between professor and student.

Inappropriate language or examples

Students are a captive audience. When you are taking a class, you have no choice but to be in the room listening to whatever the professor chooses to say. Although the principle of "academic freedom" gives professors substantial discretion over what they teach and how they explain the material, there are limits to such freedom, and students should not be subjected to comments by professors that exceed those limits.

For example, a professor should not use profanity in front of students. Few probably do, but professors may believe that some words are relatively harmless and they use them to make a point or startle students who may have stopped paying attention during a long lecture.

If a professor is quoting from literature, or a court decision, or a responsible source, it may be all right to use some profane words if the professor gives the students some warning. But hearing those words may make you uncomfortable, and your professors should not use such language as a matter of routine.

If a professor uses inappropriate language regularly, you should say something to the professor privately. Just as a professor wants to avoid humiliating students in front of the class, a student could embarrass a professor by saying, "Professor Jones, I wish you would not use that word. I find it offensive." It is something the professor needs to hear, but it is better said after class or in the office.

Professors are generally careful about examples they use, but occasionally they show a lack of sensitivity to student feelings. Some professors use passages from books, or visual depictions such as a picture or videos, that are of a sexual nature where something less controversial would have worked as well. Sometimes sexual activity and attitudes toward sex are appropriate for discussion in the class, but professors must avoid conducting the class in a way that makes students uncomfortable.

If the professor is talking about things in the class that you find offensive, say something to the professor in the office. He or she may have a good explanation for why it is necessary to use those examples, or may decide that something else could make the point that would not create problems.

Humor

Some professors are not only interesting but also amusing. When humor is used appropriately, it can make the lectures and the course more enjoyable. There is nothing wrong with a professor including an occasional humorous anecdote that is directly related to the course material.

But not surprisingly, some professors don't know where to draw the line. They tell jokes that not only seem unrelated to the course, but are potentially offensive to students. Students who think that professors waste precious class time trying to be comedians are likely to be critical of the course and will let the professor know that on the teaching evaluations at the end of the semester. Professors should also not tell off-color or sexually related jokes to students.

If a professor spends too much time trying to be funny, you could just let it pass and hope that he or she will waste less class time as the semester continues. But sometimes professors don't realize how much class time they spend talking about unimportant stuff that is unrelated to the course. Some professors, for example, waste the first five or ten minutes of every class period with banter about some issue that has nothing to do with the class, but which the professor finds interesting. If this is a problem in the class, find a way to tell the professor privately. If you feel that way about how class time is used, others in the class probably do as well.

Not treating students equally in class

A professor must treat students fairly. That means that when hands are raised, the professor should not call on some students more frequently because the teacher believes those students understand the material better, will ask good questions, and will make worthwhile comments. Other students should be included.

Sometimes professors seem to listen to students of one gender or race more carefully when they talk in class as opposed to others. If this happens, you alone or with some of your classmates should say something to the professor in his or her office. Almost all professors would then try to correct the situation.

The Professor's Office

Professors have to be particularly careful not to make you feel uncomfortable when you come to their office. Sometimes, because there is noise in the hall or because you want to discuss sensitive matters such as a grade, the professor will close the door. If it makes you feel awkward, you should ask that the door be left open.

Professors should arrange the chairs in their office so you can talk to them without being on the other side of the room, but not so close that it makes you feel apprehensive. If you are going over a research paper or exam, the professor may have to sit close to you for a few minutes so you can look together at the paper and the professor's comments. But the seating should be arranged in the office so the chairs are not awkwardly close.

Because you and the professor may be alone in the office, the professor may say things to you that he or she would not say if others were around. Although professors can candidly discuss issues related to the class, your other courses, or your career plans, they should not say inappropriate things to you just because no one else hears them.

The office itself should be the right environment for professor and student interaction. Professors like to put things on their otherwise mostly drab office walls. But they should not have posters, paintings, drawings, or other artistic depictions that you may find distasteful. A professor's free speech rights are involved to some extent, but a university office is not a private art gallery. Professors should save the more provocative or controversial works of art for their home office.

For those who have not been in a university environment, all of this may sound silly. Why, some would ask, do professors and students have to worry about whether the door is open or closed, how close they sit to each other, whether the professor said inappropriate things, or if a poster on the wall is too graphic?

The answer is that universities take these matters very seriously. You must feel completely at ease going to a professor's office without worrying that he or she will sit too close, touch you, make comments about your appearance, or do other things that make you reluctant to go back.

For professors, there may be serious consequences if they behave inappropriately. If you complain about a professor, some action will be taken. No professor wants to be called into the department chair's office to be told that you were uncomfortable because of something that he or she did or said. Because you and the professor were the only ones there at the time, there may be a dispute about what happened, and that may lead to more meetings or even an administrative hearing.

This doesn't mean a professor can't be a caring and dedicated teacher who worries about you when you are having problems and suggests solutions. A professor may give you advice or, depending on the nature of the problem, may refer you to counselors or other staff on campus. But no matter how much the professor wants to help, it is important for you and the professor to respect the nature and limits of the relationship.

Sexual Harassment

You probably won't have to worry about sexual harassment. But because it does happen and is such a serious matter, you should be prepared to deal with the situation if it should happen to you.

Every college and university has a policy protecting students and employees against sexual harassment. A professor, tenured or untenured, who sexually harasses a student, colleague, or staff member, will be terminated. If the professor is tenured, there may be a series of hearings and investigations that take a year or two, or sometimes longer, and there may be subsequent lawsuits. But if the professor committed acts that are considered sexual harassment, that professor will eventually be fired.

It is often difficult for students to recognize sexual harassment as defined by the university or by federal law. Except for the most brazen professors who initiate physical contact with their students or make explicit comments about trading grades for sex, most professors who behave inappropriately do so in subtle ways.

Students must try to recognize the difference between clear-cut efforts at sexual harassment and clumsy attempts to be amusing or other actions that, while improper, don't rise to the level of harassment.

The University of Kentucky's policy is typical of many other colleges and universities. (Administrative Regulations A.R.II-1.1-9). It states that every member of the University community is prohibited from:

> • engaging in sexual harassment;
> • retaliating against a complainant or any individual who participates in an investigation;
> • making intentionally false statements.
>
> For purposes of this Policy, sexual harassment is a form of sexual discrimination that includes unwelcome sexual advances, requests for sexual favors, or other verbal or physical actions of a sexual nature when:
>
> • submission to such conduct is made explicitly or implicitly a term or condition of an individual's employment or status in a university course, program or activity;
> • submission to or rejection of such conduct by an individual is used as a basis for an employment decision or a decision affecting an individual's status in a university course, program, or activity; or
> • such conduct is sufficiently severe or pervasive to interfere with an individual's work, academic participation or performance, or creates an intimidating, hostile or offensive working or educational environment.
>
> It is the policy of the University of Kentucky that sexual harassment of students, faculty and staff is prohibited.

Many universities have debated whether to prohibit consenting relationships between professors and students, and supervisors and their employees. This is how UK deals with this issue:

> "Conduct of an amorous or sexual nature occurring in an apparently welcome relationship may be unwelcome due to the existence of a power difference which

> restricts a subordinate's freedom to participate willingly in the relationship."

Notice the language of the third bulleted paragraph above, the one dealing with the creation of a hostile or offensive educational environment. It is because of that policy that professors need to be especially careful how they interact with students in the classroom and their office. That policy does not draw the line at solicitation of sexual favors, which is obviously prohibited. It says that professors cannot create an environment in which students feel uncomfortable.

It is sometimes subtle

You are a female student talking to your male professor in his office. During the conversation, he says something about how attractive you look today. That is the only comment he makes of a personal nature. He then moves on to subjects related to the class.

Is that sexual harassment? By itself, with nothing more, it probably isn't, although if the behavior persists, and it makes you uncomfortable, it is potentially covered by the third bulleted paragraph above. It is possible that he may not realize that professors shouldn't say such things, although that is hard to believe in an era in which all faculty are informed in various ways by the university that certain kinds of behavior will not be tolerated. But the rules are rarely so specific that professors know exactly what is acceptable and what is not.

The student in such a situation is in a difficult position. If you say to the professor that you would appreciate it if he would not comment on your appearance, you may worry that he will be offended and think that you are too sensitive and too quick to decide that you are being subjected to inappropriate behavior. That is precisely why professors shouldn't say those things to students in the first place. It puts you in an awkward position and depending on how the professor responds, it may affect your relationship. With all the things you have to worry about, this shouldn't be one of them.

Universities often publish information about sexual harassment for students to read. You may get written materials and advice from several places on campus:
- Ombudsperson's office
- University student affairs office
- University counsel's office
- Student government association
- Student government association lawyer
- Dean of students office

What You Should Do

If a professor does something in the classroom or the office that is sufficiently serious and which you can't discuss with the professor, you need to see the department chair. If you try to talk to another faculty member about it, that person is also likely to refer you to the head of the department. As mentioned before, you may also want to talk to the ombudsperson at the university.

If you are a victim of sexual harassment, you should file a formal complaint.

If you go see the professor's supervisor, you need to think about the implications. Depending on the nature of the problem, the department chair will take one or more actions. The chair may call the professor into the office for a private talk and will give the professor the chance to explain. If the matter is potentially serious and could lead to a lawsuit against the university brought by you or the professor, or administrative action against the professor, the department chair will notify the dean. The dean, in turn, may inform the university counsel's office (the university attorney), the dean of students, or other university officials. What the chair will not do is ignore your complaint.

Once you have accused a professor of sexual harassment, it will be hard to keep the news from spreading around the department. It probably won't be long before other professors and students know about your complaint. That may be embarrassing to you and the professor. As the description of the incident gets passed from one person to the other, there is an increasing chance that distortions or inaccuracies will become part of the story. You want to make sure you have legitimate reasons for reporting a professor's behavior to the department chair.

The ordeal could last years

If you file a formal complaint of sexual harassment against a professor, and you should certainly do so if the circumstances justify it, you have to be prepared to be involved in the case for one or more years. Sometimes the university's hearings and other procedures, and the lawsuit if there is one, will last well beyond the time you graduate.

Once under way, a sexual harassment investigation, and the subsequent action taken by the university or the courts, may be painful for you and your family. You will be bewildered at how cumbersome and slow the procedures are that the university has established to deal with such cases. Especially if the alleged harasser is a tenured professor, the university will appoint a committee to gather information, hear evidence from witnesses, and consider an appropriate punishment, if any. That recommendation will go to various levels of the university, eventually reaching the president's office.

Sometimes, a president will send the case back to the investigating committee to gather more information or to take additional action because the committee did not follow one of the required procedures. Eventually, although it may take several years, the president will decide the matter.

During the long investigation, you will have to tell what happened over and over again, sometimes to the panel gathering the information, and sometimes to a group that includes the professor's lawyer. You may have to retain your own counsel to protect your rights. If you do, it will almost always be at your expense.

If there is a dispute between you and the professor over what happened and the investigating committee cannot determine who is recalling the events accurately, it is unlikely that the university will take action against the professor. The facts surrounding the incident have to be relatively clear. It is often not enough for the person bringing the complaint to simply say what happened because the professor will deny the student's versions of the events. Before a professor is disciplined or fired, corroborating evidence will be needed in the form of paperwork, another person who saw the behavior, or a person who will testify that the professor did the same thing in the past.

The filing of the complaint will have serious consequences

Much is at stake here for the student and the professor. You may feel you have been victimized and want to make sure the professor won't do this again to someone else. For the professor, it may mean the end of his or her career. Few universities would hire someone who has been discharged for sexual harassment. It likely means not only the end of the professor's current income but also a lifetime prohibition on teaching. That is why the university is so careful before firing a professor, and why professors who have been dismissed for this reason often sue for monetary damages and to get their jobs back.

This is a brief discussion of what bringing a sexual harassment complaint might be like. It doesn't fully describe the expense and frustration that you may experience. You may feel that the process was stacked in favor of preserving the professor's rights with little regard for yours. For a professor who is wrongly accused, the long ordeal can be a nightmare.

It is important to say one more time that if you are a victim of harassment, you should file a complaint. The university community has a strong interest in seeing that teachers who behave this way leave the institution. But anyone who begins this process needs to know that it may last a long time, be expensive, and despite pretty solid evidence that something bad occurred, result in no punishment.

In recent years, universities have tried to change their review procedures to better protect the interests of the student, but they still generally favor the faculty member and require clear evidence that something serious happened. Some review committees are hesitant to recommend that a professor be punished if there was a single incident unless the evidence is overwhelming. If you have to show that there was a pattern of inappropriate behavior, you may have a difficult time finding former students who are willing to testify about harassment that took place some time ago.

You may end up as a defendant

If you file a formal complaint in which you say a professor committed an act of sexual harassment or created a hostile or uncomfortable environment, and the professor is fired or punished in some other way, you may be named as a defendant if the professor sues the university.

The decision to include you as a defendant may be partly due to legal strategy. It is sometimes easier to obtain testimony from parties in the case as opposed to witnesses. But the professor may also name you as a defendant to send the message that you did not tell the truth about what happened. You are likely to have to pay your own legal expenses. If you lose and the court awards damages against you, your insurance company may not pay the judgment. If the case is not overturned on appeal, you could owe the professor a substantial sum of money.

The university may try to do some things to protect you and to limit the expenses you incur in bringing the complaint. But that protection only lasts while the case is going through the university's administrative process. Once the case moves to the courts, there is little the university can do to make it less unpleasant for you.

The issues discussed in this chapter are not likely to arise during the years you are an undergraduate. You will almost certainly enjoy positive relations with your professors who behave professionally toward you and your classmates. But in case something discussed here should happen, you will have some idea what might be involved.

14

Legal Issues

Summary: This chapter discusses some legal issues and how to avoid potential problems.

Why It Matters: It is important for college students to understand their legal rights and responsibilities.

As a student, you have legal rights that may become important if something goes wrong while you are enrolled at a university. You also have legal responsibilities. Knowing a little about those rights and responsibilities may help you and your parents avoid serious problems.

You are likely to attend four years or more of college without having to deal with any of the subjects discussed in this chapter. However, it makes sense to be prepared in advance in case a difficult situation develops.

This chapter is not giving you legal advice. If you encounter circumstances that raise legal issues, you and your parents should consult a licensed attorney. The sole purpose here is to provide information that may help you understand some legal matters related to attending a college or university.

Loss of Financial Aid

Several years ago, Congress amended the law related to eligibility for federal financial aid programs. After Congress made those changes, the U.S. Department of Education wrote rules to implement the new sections of the law. One of the most controversial aspects was the one dealing with students who are convicted of drug offenses.

Congress apparently wanted students who had *previously* been convicted of a drug offense not to be eligible for federal financial aid in the form of student loans or grants. However, the Department of Education, when writing rules to implement the law, interpreted it to mean that a student who is convicted of a drug offense while receiving financial aid will lose that aid. For some students and their families, the end of such financial support would make continuing in college very difficult.

At a time when many legislatures, prosecutors and judges have become more tolerant of personal possession of small amounts of drugs, it may surprise you to learn that conviction for having even a small amount of marijuana or some other illegal drug could have such serious consequences. If you are studying at an expensive college, the loss of federal loans and grants may mean you will have to transfer to another school. Because of your drug conviction, you would not be eligible for financial aid at the new college.

Some members of Congress believe that the Department of Education misinterpreted congressional intent. They say they wanted to prohibit students with a drug conviction in their past from receiving financial aid in the first place, but that Congress did not intend for financial aid to be taken away from students once they are receiving it if they are convicted of minor drug offenses. (See "43,000 Students With

Drug Convictions Face Denial of Aid," *New York Times*, Associated Press, Dec. 29, 2001, p. A8; and Arlene Levinson, "34,000 financial-aid applicants may not receive federal funding," *Lexington Herald-Leader*, July 15, 2001, p. A12).

The lesson here is obvious. Think about what it would mean for your college plans and your parents' financial status if you were prohibited from receiving financial aid because you got caught using drugs.

Student Records

All colleges and universities must comply with an important federal law that governs student records. It is called the Family Educational Rights and Privacy Act of 1974 (FERPA).

Most universities explain the most relevant sections of the law in the bulletin or at the front of the schedule of classes. You should take a few minutes to look over the description of the law.

The key sections explain what student records are and that the information in those records must be accurate. If you believe something in your files is incorrect, you have the right to challenge it.

Once you notify the university in writing that you want to see your files, the university has 45 days to comply. Various units of the university may have student records. For example, there may be files on you in the department, the college, and at the university level. If you have concerns about the information in those records, you need to check all of them.

If you challenge any of the records, and the university does not agree to amend them, you can request a hearing before a grievance committee. If the committee rules in your favor, the records will be changed.

The law also limits what kind of information can be released about you. Generally, universities can only disclose "directory" information that you have agreed can be disseminated to others. But no other information is supposed to be

released. For example, a professor is not supposed to ac-
knowledge to anyone outside the university that you are in a
class unless you have given your consent. There are exceptions to the disclosure requirement but they are generally
protective of your rights.

Because the university has a lot of private information about
you, it must handle your records properly. If you have any concerns about this, talk to the appropriate university official.

Legal Rights at a Public University

When it comes to legal rights, students at public universities have some advantages. Unfortunately, there are some important disadvantages, and one of the most significant has to
do with your ability to sue a public university if you are injured while a student.

For complicated legal and historical reasons, states enjoy
what is called "sovereign immunity." That means that under
most circumstances, a state cannot be sued unless it has explicitly waived that immunity. The idea is to protect public
funds and public property from lawsuits whose judgments
would have to be paid with taxpayer money.

Depending on a number of factors—such as the relationship between the public college or university and the state and
how much of its budget it receives from the state legislature—a
public institution of higher education is likely to be considered
an "arm of the state" and thus protected by sovereign immunity. That means that even when university employees are
clearly at fault, you cannot sue the university itself. You may be
able to sue its officials, but that is hard to do successfully.

The 11th Amendment

The 11th Amendment to the U.S. Constitution makes it
very difficult to sue a *public university* if you are injured.

Originally that amendment was intended to protect a state from being sued by the citizen of another state in federal court. In other words, if you were a resident of Kentucky, you could not sue the state of Virginia in federal court.

But in 1890, for reasons that remain controversial to this day, the Supreme Court extended that protection to lawsuits brought by citizens against their own state. That means that if you are a citizen of Kentucky, you can't sue the state of Kentucky in federal court even if you were injured through the negligence of one of its officials.

Some exceptions to this principle are complicated. Sometimes you can sue in federal court if Congress, when passing a law that grants you some rights or protections, explicitly says that it intended to permit such lawsuits. For this exception to work, Congress has to have clearly "abrogated" the state's sovereign immunity. But even then, the courts may not permit the lawsuit to proceed. Sometimes you can sue if, through one of its actions, the state waived or partially waived its sovereign immunity and thus agreed to be sued.

However, the Supreme Court in 1996 handed down a ruling that makes it even more difficult than it has been in the recent past to sue a state in federal court. There is much more to this issue, but it is enough to say that if you are injured and want to sue the university in federal court, you are likely to have a tough time.

State versus federal court

You may have noticed that up to this point, the discussion has focused on suing in federal court. If you cannot sue in federal court because of the nature of your lawsuit, you may be able to bring your action in state court.

Federal and state courts operate under different rules and often apply different laws. If your rights have been violated while you are a student at a university and those rights are based on federal laws or the federal Constitution, you have the opportunity to sue in federal court. Generally you would be better off suing in federal rather than state court. There are many reasons for this and they don't apply in every case. But if you are trying to bring a lawsuit against your state and the taxpayers will have to pay if you win, the procedures that a federal court follows and the laws under which you sue are likely to be more favorable in federal court.

States have their own procedures

If you are shut out of federal court because of Supreme Court decisions, you may think that a state court would be available to hear your lawsuit. In most cases, you would be wrong.

In Kentucky, for example, you cannot sue the state in state court. You have to file a claim with an administrative body created by the legislature called the "Board of Claims." The board then decides whether the claim has merit. The maximum amount the board can award you is $100,000. That is small considering the harm you may have suffered because of the negligence of the university's employees. You have no choice but to go through the Board of Claims. You cannot sue the state in court and will not get the chance to make your case before a judge and jury. Some other states have similar requirements.

Suing university employees

If you are injured through a negligent act on the part of a university official, or if you are deprived of rights to which you were entitled, you may be able to sue the employees who were responsible, even though you can't sue the university itself. In such a situation, the university usually doesn't abandon its employees. It will probably pay their legal bills and if the jury awards you money, it will probably pay the judgment.

However, it may be very difficult for you to get to court if you sue a university official. That is because as with the state, university employees are likely to be immune from such lawsuits if the dispute is related to the performance of their official duties.

Before discussing whether you may be able to sue a university administrator, professor, or another employee, you need to know about a law enacted many years ago. Congress passed a very important law in 1871 to allow people to sue a state official for depriving them of any "rights, privileges or immunities secured by the Constitution and laws." The law has permitted people injured by the actions of state officials to sue them.

But those officials often enjoy immunity, just as the state does.

Here is how such immunity works: It is not enough to show that a staff member or professor did something, or failed to do something, that led to your being injured or deprived of your rights. You also have to prove that the action, or failure to act, was *not* within the usual discretion granted to a person in that position. Instead, you would have to show that the person was performing a "ministerial" act, meaning an act carrying out an official duty that doesn't depend on the person exercising discretion or judgment.

> **It is very hard to bring a successful lawsuit against a public university or its employees.**

Why have the courts and legislatures developed this standard? The theory is that public officials should not be dragged into court whenever they take action that displeases someone. If that happened, they would not be able to do their jobs. The courts believe that officials must be given substantial leeway when performing their duties, and that they should not be held accountable except when they knew or should have known that they were violating "clearly established rights."

Only when officials are performing ministerial duties over which they have no discretion do you have the opportunity to sue in some states. But even then, those lawsuits are difficult to pursue successfully.

This has all been a bit legalistic, but it basically means two things:

> First, if you are injured or deprived of your rights at a *public university*, you will most likely not be able to sue the university itself because of the 11th Amendment.
>
> Second, you probably will have a difficult time suing the administrator or professor who was most responsible for your injury or loss of rights because that university employee was likely exercising discretionary judgment and therefore enjoys immunity.

How immunity issues may arise

Let's say the public university you attend is located in a part of the country where it snows. You are walking across the campus on a winter day and slip on ice on the steps leading to the building where you have class. You fall down and badly injure your back.

Because the university enjoys "sovereign immunity," you cannot sue the university itself for your injury. You then try to sue the person who is in charge of making sure the campus is cleared of snow and ice on walkways and steps. But unless that person or a subordinate had been told that there was a dangerous build-up of ice on those stairs, and that the failure to correct the situation was not a reasonable exercise of discretion, you will not be able to sue.

To prevent your lawsuit from proceeding, all the university employee has to say is that it is impossible to clear every walkway and the steps of every building soon after it snows or ice forms. Decisions have to be made, and thus discretion exercised, about where to deploy workers for such purposes. If the person makes that statement, the judge is likely to dismiss the lawsuit.

Accidents like this may not be avoidable, but knowing that you probably can't sue the university or its officials may encourage you and your parents to carry appropriate medical insurance, including disability coverage, in case you are injured in such a situation and cannot go back to school or work.

Make sure you have adequate insurance coverage while you are attending a university.

Legal Rights at a Private University

Most students will attend a private college or university without ever realizing that they and their professors do not enjoy the same rights as students and professors at a public university. The reason for the difference is that the U.S. Constitution applies to government, but not private entities.

Here is how it makes a difference: If you are a student at a private university, and want to hand out a pamphlet protesting some government action or university policy, officials at the private university can stop you from doing so. Or if you create a Web site using the university's server that criticizes the university, it can shut down your site.

But don't you have a First Amendment right to hand out literature, or establish a Web site, or to peaceably demonstrate, or undertake other expressive activities? The answer is no if you attend a private college because the First Amendment and the entire Constitution apply only to government, not to non-governmental entities such as a private university.

Not only are you not entitled to rights granted under the First Amendment, you receive no substantive or procedural rights under the 14th Amendment. That means private universities will decide what procedures they must follow before you can be suspended, expelled, or punished in some other way, or a professor can be fired. They do not have to bother with the section of the 14th Amendment that talks about "due process of law."

Private universities
can't ignore the law

If you attend a private university, you still have legal protections, but those protections are established in statutes —laws passed by state legislatures and Congress—not grounded in the Constitution. For example, private universities can discriminate on the basis of race, gender or religion. But they are prohibited from doing so not because of the "equal protection" clause of the 14th Amendment of the Constitution. It is because of federal laws that prohibit discrimination.

There are, however, limits on the rights that Congress can protect through federal laws and limited remedies that it can provide. In order for such laws to survive a constitutional challenge, they have to be related in some way to interstate commerce or be based on some other provision of the Constitution. In recent years, some courts have been aggressively striking down federal laws that they believe interfere with the autonomy of the states. That means it may be harder to sue a private university using a federal law than it has been in the past. You may still be able to sue in state court based on a state law, but as explained before, some states limit your access to court and how much you can be compensated.

Sororities and Fraternities

Parties at sororities and fraternities sometimes get out of control. You may consume too much alcohol or use an illegal drug that has an unintended effect. Someone may put something in your drink without your knowledge, and you may suffer an injury as a result.

If you are harmed in a hazing incident, are a victim of date rape while at a sorority or fraternity house, or something else bad happens to you there, you will find that it is difficult to sue the national organization of that sorority or fraternity. Those organizations often have been able to argue successfully in court that they are not responsible for the actions of members of individual chapters. Only when those organizations have been on notice over an extended period that there are dangerous hazing rituals or some other problem at a particular chapter, and they take no action to prevent further problems, do you have any hope of defeating them in court.

If the sorority or fraternity house is not on campus, you will also have a very tough time suing university officials. In order to maintain such a lawsuit, you would have to clearly demonstrate that the university knew there was a potentially dangerous situation developing at an off-campus sorority or fraternity house and that they failed to take appropriate action. Those are very difficult standards to meet in court.

**It is very hard to sue the
national organization of a sorority or fraternity.
You may be able to sue only the individuals
involved in the incident that led to your injury.**

If you have been a victim of hazing or date rape, a prosecutor may bring a criminal action against those who allegedly committed illegal acts. But the requirement that a jury be convinced "beyond a reasonable doubt" of the guilt of the defendants makes obtaining convictions difficult.

Some victims, therefore, must file civil suits to be compensated for the harm they have suffered. In such actions, the legal standard is easier to prove than in criminal cases. However, because you can't sue the national organization, you may be limited to bringing a lawsuit against the student officers of the sorority or fraternity or anyone else who was part of the hazing. When it comes to date rape, it would mean suing the perpetrator.

But those individuals are likely to have limited assets to pay a judgment. Under some circumstances, if their parents' homeowners insurance has a liability policy that covers the child at a university, it is possible you could collect a judgment from their insurance company. But that may depend on whether the jury decides the person who injured you acted "negligently" or "intentionally."

The reasons are complicated, but basically many liability insurance policies will not cover reckless or intentional acts. They will cover only actions that are more "accidental" in nature. This leads to an ironic and frustrating situation for the person injured. If someone intended to injure you and it was not just negligence on his or her part, you are not likely to collect any money from the person's insurance company.

Date Rape

This is a serious matter and you need to think about how to protect yourself in advance. Date rape can happen with little or no warning in a place where you would expect to be safe. The act can be committed by someone whom you trust.

Probably a substantial percentage of date rapes happen when one or both of the individuals have been drinking or using drugs. They may not be able to exercise the same judgment they would if they were sober or not under the influence of illegal substances.

Perhaps this will sound like obvious advice, but you should avoid the possibility of being a date rape victim by not putting yourself in that situation. Anytime you are drinking or using drugs that may have effects on you that you never intended or have never experienced before, you run the risk of being a victim.

Date rape cases are very difficult to prosecute. One person will say the sexual activity was consensual, while the other will not. Unless there is evidence beyond differing interpretations of the incident, it is likely that a prosecutor will not pursue a criminal case.

As mentioned previously, you may be able to sue the person you accuse of rape, and because the standard for winning is less stringent than that required for a criminal conviction, it is possible you could be awarded damages by a court. But just as juries in criminal cases need clear evidence that a crime has been committed, a civil trial jury would have to see substantial proof that a sexual assault has taken place. And once again, you have to consider whether it is worth the thousands of dollars it takes to sue if the defendant has little money to pay the judgment.

Your parents have probably already talked to you about these matters. But you may forget that advice when you are surrounded by the excitement and fun of a lively party and meeting new people.

If you believe you are a victim of date rape, contact the appropriate authorities or a rape crisis center and don't do anything that destroys evidence. There are experienced people in the community who will tell you what you need to do. If you contaminate evidence or wait too long to report the incident, it will be much more difficult to bring a criminal prosecution or a civil suit against the perpetrator.

Landlord-Tenant Issues

Before moving to an off-campus house or apartment, you should know the basics of the landlord-tenant laws.

Those laws will often govern what the landlord can put in the lease, how much refundable and non-refundable deposit can be collected, the circumstances under which you can get that deposit back, when you can be evicted, how much notice you must give, and other important issues. Such laws may apply statewide or may be local in nature.

Unfortunately, there is usually no single place where you can easily obtain that information. You may be able to go to the Web site for the state or local government and find all the laws related to landlord-tenant issues. Or you may find a book on the shelves at a local bookstore that will outline the laws. It is also possible that the student government association hired an attorney to collect those laws in a small booklet and you will be able to get the information that way. There may also be other organizations that help tenants with landlord-tenant disputes.

Considering how much your deposit and rent are likely to be, it may be worth $50 or $100 for you to briefly talk to an attorney about the lease you are going to sign and what your rights are under the law. Sometimes students sign leases that appear to force them to give up rights to which they are entitled under the law. For example, the state or local law may prohibit a non-refundable deposit, yet the lease requires you to provide that additional money before you move in.

You may have to threaten to take the landlord to small-claims court after you move out in order to get your deposit back, but knowing the law is the first step.

Some landlords have tenants sign leases that say they are responsible for the entire period of the lease even if they leave the property early. But what they don't tell you is that the state or local law likely says you are only responsible for the rent while the place is vacant and that the landlord has to make a good-faith effort to re-rent it. Once the place is occupied again, you are no longer responsible. You may have to go to small-claims court to get those months of rent back from the landlord.

There are many other potential problems that could arise in a landlord-tenant relationship. It is extremely important for you to understand the law and what you are agreeing to in the lease.

Renters Insurance

Before leaving for college, or if you are a university student already, you should know whether your possessions are covered by your parents' homeowners insurance policy when you move into a dorm or an off-campus house or apartment. If you are not covered, you can buy insurance for very little money.

A renter's insurance policy with a limit of, let's say, $25,000 and liability coverage (protection if someone sues you while injured on the premises) of $100,000 costs about $175 per year. That's 47 cents a day over a 12-month period.

Some students may think that they only have a few possessions, including a computer and their clothes, and they don't need insurance. But sometimes they don't think about what would happen to them if the house where they lived with several friends were to sustain fire damage, and no one could live there for a while. The insurance would pay some of the expenses of having to live elsewhere until the house is repaired.

Medical and Car Insurance

Check to see if you are covered by your parents' medical insurance and car insurance. Be sure to ask this: Do you have to be a full-time student in order to be covered by that insurance? If so, does the insurance company or the university decide what is full-time status?

Previously, I recommended that you consider taking no more than 12 credits (as opposed to a normal load of 15 in a semester) if you have especially difficult courses or if you have to work a lot of hours a week.

If you start out taking 12 credits, and have to drop a class, you may go to part-time status. If that happens, it is possible that you will no longer be covered by your family's medical insurance and car insurance. If you don't check in advance, you may only find that out after you have become ill or have been involved in a car accident.

Crime Statistics

Under a federal law passed in 1998, public and private colleges and universities must keep and report statistics on what crimes have been committed on or near their campuses. Besides keeping the records themselves, they report those statistics to the state, the FBI, and the U.S. Department of Education.

There are a number of ways to find out about crimes on college campuses. The easiest is probably to go to the Department of Education's Web site at <www.ed.gov>. You will see links to the crime statistics for the more than 600 colleges and universities that report to the department. You will find a lot of information at the site.

Colleges and universities are expected to report all incidences of homicide, manslaughter, sex offenses, robbery, aggravated assault, burglary, motor vehicle theft and arson, and hate crimes. They are also required to report separate statistics for each campus and say where the crime occurred.

You will also see statistics on illegal weapons possession and liquor and drug law violations, including the number of persons referred to the campus administration for disciplinary action for these violations.

You and your parents will want to be informed about criminal activity on or near the campus, but statistics may not give you a complete picture. Sometimes campus police departments characterize certain crimes in a way that is misleading and makes the crime seem less serious than it was. They don't want the campus to get a reputation for being a dangerous place. Remember, you should always be careful where you go and be aware that crime can happen anywhere.

Afterword

Your college years can be among the most exciting and interesting times in your life. They go by quickly, so make the most of them.

If this book has served its purpose, you and your parents will be better prepared for your undergraduate experience, and you will approach your studies in a way that will make that experience last beyond graduation.

Good luck to you and your parents as you begin or continue this important phase of your life.

Index

About the Author

Richard Labunski has been a university professor for more than 20 years. He is currently an associate professor in the School of Journalism and Telecommunications at the University of Kentucky where he teaches media law, the First Amendment and new technology, and broadcast journalism. He has also taught at the University of California, Santa Barbara; the University of Nevada, Reno; Penn State University; and the University of Washington. He has a B.A. in political science from the University of California, Berkeley, and an M.A. and Ph.D. in political science from the University of California, Santa Barbara. His J.D. is from Seattle University School of Law. He is the author of three previous books, law review articles, and newspaper commentaries. He worked for ten years in radio and TV news and has been an expert witness in First Amendment cases.

Also by Richard Labunski and available from Marley and Beck Press:

The Second Constitutional Convention:
How The American People Can
Take Back Their Government

For more information about *The Second Constitutional Convention* and *The Educated Student,* visit our Web site at: www.marleyandbeck.com

To order copies of either book, check your local bookstore or order through the Marley and Beck Web site.